Michael Donaldson

Lydia Ko

Portrait of a teen golfing sensation

PENGUIN BOOKS

PENGUIN

UK | USA | Canada | Ireland | Australia
India | New Zealand | South Africa | China

Penguin is an imprint of the Penguin Random House group of companies, whose addresses can be found at global.penguinrandomhouse.com.

Penguin Random House New Zealand

First published by Penguin Random House New Zealand, 2016

10 9 8 7 6 5 4 3 2

Cover design by Sam Bunny and Kate Barraclough © Penguin Random House New Zealand
Text design by Kate Barraclough © Penguin Random House New Zealand
Cover photographs by Photosport
Front cover background by iStock.com/LiliGraphie
Prepress by Image Centre Group
Printed and bound in Australia by Griffin Press,
an Accredited ISO AS/NZS 14001 Environmental Management Systems Printer

A catalogue record for this book is available from the National Library of New Zealand.

ISBN 978-0-14-357429-3
eISBN 978-1-74-348728-0

penguin.co.nz

MIX
Paper | Supporting responsible forestry
FSC® C018684
FSC www.fsc.org

Contents

Prologue

Pitch perfect

Lydia Ko stands on the 18th fairway of the Mission Hills Country Club in the resort city of Rancho Mirage, California — a prestigious club known as the spiritual home of women's golf.

It's her last hole in the final round of the ANA Inspiration, one of the five major championships of professional women's golf, and the first of 2016. She is tied for the lead. To win she knows she must make a birdie.

To make a birdie she must hit her ball over water, but she cannot afford to fly it too far, as the green will reject a shot played too long.

For this shot she needs the precision of a jeweller and the mind of a mathematician.

As Lydia surveys her ball, caddy Jason Hamilton rattles off a series of numbers like someone calling bingo. And the conversation that follows is reminiscent of an astronaut talking to NASA mission control as they calculate a lunar landing.

'Sixty-one, twenty-eight, eighty-nine . . .'

'How much behind?' asks Lydia.

'About four behind to the bottom of the slope and nine in total.'

'Eighty-nine pin?'

'Yeah, about six short of the pin with slight downhill. So that's eighty-three and slightly downhill.'

'Eighty-four?'

'Yeah, that's all you need, eighty-four.'

'Wind helping?'

'Yeah, see the flags behind the green, there's a little bit of help, probably about three yards.'

'Eighty-one?'

'Yeah, and adjusted, seventy-nine. You wanna land about half a yard left and spin to the pin.'

'Go right at it?'

'Yep.'

Translated, the conversation between golfer and caddy means this:

Lydia faces a carry of 61 yards over water in front of the green with the hole located a further 28 yards past that point, for a total of 89 yards. She has 4 yards, roughly, as a backstop to the top of a slope, with a total of 9 yards to the back of the green.

Hamilton then reckons she needs to land the ball 6 yards short of the flag, knowing it will then make one big bounce.

Lydia asks whether the wind is helping — it is, and it will carry the ball an additional 3 yards by Hamilton's reckoning. So to land it at the precise point desired, based on the information he is feeding, she has to swing as if hitting the shot 81 yards.

He then makes an adjustment for the fact the green is downhill relative to their current position and comes up with 79 yards as the distance she's aiming for.

All this is going on as Lydia practises her rhythmic, fluid swing, trying to sense exactly how hard to hit the ball to get the distance her caddy has calculated.

As well, she needs to aim half a yard to the left of the pin because of the slight side-spin she will put on the ball and the fact the slope will kick the ball left. It's all about feel, drawn from the experience of hitting countless golf balls for 14 of her nearly 19 years.

Lydia stands behind the ball for a couple of seconds, picks her target, walks to the ball and, after a short practice swing to make sure the club is going back on the right line, without fuss, she swings.

Chapter One
A Se Ri kid

Women's golf changed forever the moment a young Korean named Se Ri Pak took the world by storm in 1998.

She had been a dominant player on the Korean women's tour in 1996 and 1997, and when she joined the Ladies Professional Golf Association (LPGA) circuit as a 20-year-old in 1998 she did so at a time when golf was going through a once-in-a-hundred-years revolution thanks to a young American with ties to Asia: Tiger Woods.

Woods redefined golf with his runaway Masters tournament victory of 1997, becoming a superstar — especially in Asia, thanks to his mother, Kultida, being Thai. He also changed the appetite for golf on television and with it the prizemoney in the men's game.

But there's no denying the LPGA also benefited from the light emanating from Woods' halo. Se Ri Pak could not have picked a better time to venture onto the global stage.

Woods' story was one defined by a domineering father and Se Ri's story was no different, as with many other superstars of her era. Like Woods, tennis sisters Serena and Venus Williams and Andre Agassi, among countless others, the young Korean was driven by the same force behind many a young star — a determined father.

And when it comes to tough fathers, Joon Chul Pak left Earl Woods, Richard Williams and Mike Agassi in his wake.

While Earl Woods used his military background as a Green Beret to toughen up a young Tiger for life on the Professional Golfers Association (PGA) Tour, Joon Chul Pak drew on his self-confessed background as a one-time gangster to do the same with his daughter.

Happy to show off knife scars from stab wounds inflicted during his life in South Korea's underworld, Pak, a self-described 'thug' with a love of golf, saw a glimmer of talent in his 11-year-old daughter when she tagged along to the driving range one day.

From then on he made it his life's mission to turn her into a superstar. There are stories of Se Ri practising in freezing conditions, with icicles forming in her hair; of tears during midnight sessions on the range as she tried to perfect a shot; of not wanting (or being allowed) to sleep until she executed the ideal ball flight. But the story that followed Se Ri Pak to America was of the times her father left her alone in a cemetery at night with only ghosts for company.

Whether Joon Chul Pak borrowed the cemetery routine from someone else or dreamt it up himself is not certain, but it's not uncommon to hear of South Korean athletes spending nights among the tombstones; the South Korean archery team preparing for the 2012 London Olympics reportedly used the same tactic.

The idea is to conquer fear and build a tough mind, and it's quite a demand on a teenage girl to have her spend a night alone surrounded by the dead and her own thoughts. One night, aged 16, Se Ri told her father the graveyard no longer terrified her — in fact, she was happy there. 'And then I knew her heart was strong,' Joon Chul said in a *New York Times* report. 'We never went back to the cemetery.'

In 1998, Joon Chul's tactics — and Se Ri's determination to achieve the goals set by her father — paid a handsome dividend. She won two major championships in a single season and at 20 years old became the youngest woman to win multiple golf majors.

Se Ri went on to count five major golf championships among her 39 wins in total. *Golf World* writer Eric Adelson, in a 2008 tribute celebrating Se Ri's 10 years on the LPGA tour, called her 'a pioneer . . . who changed the face of golf even more than Tiger Woods'.

Se Ri was a pioneer because when she came to the LPGA in 1998, she was the only Korean player. Ten years later, she took her place as one of 45 Koreans on the women's professional circuit. Her countrywomen now dominate world golf. Perhaps Se Ri's greatest legacy is the fact the single largest source of revenue for the LPGA is the sale of TV rights in South Korea. Her success, at a period when Korea's economy started to boom and leisure pursuits such as golf gained favour, couldn't have been better timed. She single-handedly boosted the profile of golf in her country and inspired an army of young girls to start to wield golf weaponry.

But it wasn't just a successful role model that inspired the wave of Korean women who have colonised world golf. If all it took was role models, Tiger Woods' dominance of men's golf in the United States should have created a generation of African-American golfers.

While many academics and newspaper writers have tried to explain the golf success of Korean women by focusing on work ethic, there are a range of influences to be considered. In a 2004 academic paper entitled 'Culture, Gender Roles, and Sport: The Case of Korean Players on the LPGA Tour', written by Eui Hang Shin and Edward Adam Nam and published in the *Journal of Sport and Social Issues* in August 2004, some fascinating insights emerged.

Shin argued the success of female Korean golfers was due to a number of cultural and social factors, including: a disposition towards meditation and inner calm; a resilience among Korean women; the close father–daughter relationship in which fathers are indulgent of their daughters; the demanding education system and the resultant pressure on children to study day and night to achieve their goals; and the rising status of golf in Korea and its acceptance as an area where women could excel, having had other channels blocked in male-dominated society.

'Golf requires calm and mental strength balanced with the willingness to take risks. From Shamanism to Buddhism to Confucianism and even to Christianity, Koreans have traditionally sought meditation and the search for inner calm,' the authors wrote.

This almost mystical sounding disposition is juxtaposed with a Korean passion for gambling — or rather, well-calculated risk-taking illustrated by the all-or-nothing approach to the civil service/judiciary bar examination. The exam is open to anyone, but only one per cent pass. Failure is common but the reward is life-altering in a 'credential-based society'.

In the stifling golf arena, having an ability to calm the mind under pressure while taking calculated risks with hundreds of thousands of dollars on the line has seen Koreans fearlessly succeed where others crumble.

Golf doesn't necessarily require great physical strength or size — especially in the women's arena — so the Korean penchant for practice can also make a difference.

Se Ri Pak's midnight practice sessions were an embodiment of a well-recognised work ethic existing in Korean society. To do well at school ensures access to the best university education and therefore a top job in prized careers such as law or medicine. As a result, school days are followed by night schools, also known as cram schools or academies, with children often getting home after 10 pm, when they squeeze in homework before a 12.30 am bedtime. Private tutors are fitted in around the margins of study-crammed days. Se Ri Pak had this attitude; it's just that she spent her nights at a driving range rather than in study.

With this expectation of, and appetite for, hard work, when it comes to high-pressure contests, Korean golfers are regarded as having the mental toughness to cope. They've been competing all their lives in a frantic bid to be among the elite.

As Shin's study noted, the 'exam hell' Korean children endure requires 'practice, practice, practice. That's why you see these kids are determined to practise their golf swing day after day.'

Curiously, there's also a cultural trait which may serve Koreans on the golf course — an expectation that they don't smile in public. Maintaining an expression of neutrality or even a frown is regarded as important in Korean society. As a result, Korean women can appear impervious to pressure — they simply show no emotion — which can be unsettling for their rivals. TV golf commentator Judy Rankin illustrated it by saying: 'Controlling your emotions, not being open about your emotions — Asian culture views that kind of control as a strength.'

Perhaps key to the unprecedented success of Koreans on the fairways of the world is the close involvement of their parents.

The inner workings of the Korean family are much different from a typical western family. Relationships between children and parents are close and intimate. Parents are expected to devote themselves to building an emotional and financial base from which their children can follow their own dreams.

In return parents are given the utmost respect and are obeyed without question. 'It is not that Korean families do not emphasise independence and self-awareness. Rather, once dreams and goals are made, parents are present to direct their children in the right direction and provide the tools necessary to succeed at any cost,' said Shin's study.

When a child picks and commits to a career route, the parents bet everything they've got on that goal. What's more, it's common for Korean families to plan a child's education up to 10 years into the future. A successful career is mapped out from the earliest years; after all, if you're betting everything on a single track to success, you'd better make sure there's a blueprint.

Again, this thinking can be seen in Se Ri Pak's achievements. When asked about normal teenage behaviours such as going to movies and dating boyfriends, Se Ri's father told the *New York Times*: 'Ten years from now. Golf now, that later.'

It is estimated a decade-long dedication to a child's golfing dream could cost at least half a million US dollars — a figure, we shall discover, accurately reflected in Lydia Ko's amateur career — so once Korean parents commit to golf as a career path for their daughters they don't want to hold back, as it

A decade-long dedication to a child's golfing dream could cost at least half a million US dollars — a figure accurately reflected in Lydia Ko's amateur career.

would be a shame to throw away all that effort and money by giving up too soon.

And in the past 20 years it has been daughters rather than sons returning the family's investment in golf. This is partly due to Se Ri Pak's influence, but also because in Korea sons are expected to aim higher than a sporting career. Plus, young men must serve a mandatory two years in the military forces, which puts their lives and career paths on hold. This happened recently to aspiring male pro Sang Moon Bae, whose promising career — and earning potential — hit a brick wall in 2015 when he had to quit the PGA Tour to carry out his military service. Women don't have this requirement, allowing the family to invest more heavily in their golf career.

Se Ri Pak's former manager, Steven Kil, once said: 'Korean fathers have come to see golf as a good and respected career for their daughters.'

Soon after Pak took the golf world by storm in 1998, junior female golfers flooded the system, leading to the creation of numerous golf academies. The ensuing golf boom served only to increase the number of brilliant young Korean women golfers coming off the production line.

Around the time Se Ri Pak burst onto the global golf scene as a bona fide superstar, Gil Hong Ko and Bon Sook (Tina) Hyon's second daughter, Bogyung, was born in Seoul on 24 April 1997. The meaning of Korean names is usually taken from the Chinese characters and in this case Bogyung means 'precious gem' or 'jade'.

When the family moved to New Zealand they chose an English name for their daughter to avoid mispronunciations or confusion. As a Catholic family, they followed a tradition of taking biblical names, with Lydia being one of the few female names in the New Testament.

That precious gem, whom the world would come to know as Lydia Ko, took her first steps in a golf-mad Korean environment tailor-made for young girls to succeed.

Like any South Korean girl born in the last few years of the twentieth century, Lydia was destined to grow up revering Se Ri Pak. Such was Se Ri's magnetism that Lydia's dad took her to a golf tournament to watch the Korean heroine play. It was a profound experience for Lydia to see this legend first hand, and she was mesmerised by Se Ri's ability to make a little white ball fly through the sky and by how the crowd adored her.

At the time the golf bug was biting, Lydia's family took a holiday to Sydney, Australia, to visit relatives. There, five-year-old Lydia was gifted a seven-iron and a putter by her aunt, Insook Hyon, an academic.

Armed with her new tools, and describing herself as a 'Se Ri kid', Lydia joined thousands of other young girls on a journey to emulate her hero. Like so many Se Ri kids, however, initially the closest she got to the actual sport of golf was the inside of a driving range.

With a growing addiction to making that ball fly, Lydia went day after day to the driving range on Jeju Island, a province of South Korea to which the family had moved from Seoul. Jeju lies south of the mainland and Lydia once described it as South Korea's Stewart Island — a small island off the southern tip of New Zealand.

While she was just one of thousands of Se Ri kids, she did stand out, drawing attention to herself with her uncanny ability to clip the ball off the fake grass mat and into the distance.

'People stopped to watch,' noted Lydia. 'They said, "You're good. You're very good." I thought, "Well, then, I must be good."

My father doesn't play golf, but he noticed the comments. He began training me.'

Like thousands of other parents whose daughters had caught the golf bug, Lydia's mum and dad wanted to make sure she had the best chance to succeed, even at five years old. So rather than just Gil Hong being in the driving seat, both parents took an active role in building their daughter's small foothold in the new sport.

Tina, in typical Korean fashion, looked for someone to teach Lydia the basics. But the first professional she approached rebuffed her, saying Lydia was too young and she wouldn't understand his instructions.

Unfazed, Tina offered him more money to take on the challenge. That little extra push would become an important part of the Lydia Ko story, in which a series of small pushes created a force capable of knocking down some of the oldest walls in golf.

Day after day — she reportedly once hit golf balls for 50 days in a row — as Lydia swung her aunt's seven-iron at an indoor driving range under the eye of a reluctant tutor, her parents reopened discussions about leaving the hustle and bustle of South Korea for a new life overseas.

But where do you take a six-year-old with a penchant for golf? They hadn't yet hatched a plan to make Lydia into a professional, but they wanted to live in a country where opportunities to play golf readily existed. They also had to think of their other daughter Sura, a teenager already studying in Canada.

For many years Koreans had headed to the United States for education and career-building, so North America was on the radar. So too Australia . . . and New Zealand.

They mulled it over and decided the wide open spaces of

Canada would be a great place for the family of a young golfer. However, bureaucratic red tape meant emigration to Canada was a more demanding process than gaining entry to New Zealand. Throughout Lydia's life, being in the right place at the right time has been crucial, and the decision to abandon Canada and opt for New Zealand proved to be one of those moments.

Chapter Two

Hothouse flower

When the Ko family arrived in Auckland in 2003 they landed in the perfect environment for an aspiring young golfer, a ready-made hothouse into which they could plant the seed of their daughter's emerging talent. From the supportive Korean subculture with a love of golf, to a relaxed Kiwi school system, and a landscape dotted with facilities — everything Lydia needed for her golfing development was close at hand.

Surfing in on a second wave of Korean migration — the first wave had been halted by anti-Asian sentiment in the mid-1990s, coupled with an Asian economic downturn in the late '90s — they arrived into an established ethnic precinct, a mini-Korea of about 40,000 who were affluent, skilled, well-connected and often devoted to golf. It was a safe, secure, supportive, almost self-sufficient environment in a region with plenty of golf courses.

Golf was the primary leisure pursuit of a community which had time, money and an inclination to enjoy the opportunities that came with the New Zealand lifestyle. This was the new face of New Zealand migration, built on the back of policy changes in the late 1980s which did away with a system that favoured migrants from selected countries.

The country system was abolished in favour of a points system, similar to Canada's but more user-friendly it seems, which targeted skilled and wealthy people from anywhere in the world.

Skilled Asian migrants who came to New Zealand in the 1990s did so with a lot of capital, says Distinguished Professor Paul Spoonley of Massey University. They sought not just to establish new businesses but also to enjoy the lifestyle. 'I refer to it as a semi-retirement migration,' Spoonley says. 'They were immersed in leisure activities and for Koreans golf was right at the forefront of that.'

When the Ko family landed, New Zealand was also over the worst of the 1990s anti-Asian sentiment as espoused by the policies of Winston Peters' New Zealand First party and summed up by the 1993 story entitled 'Inv-Asian' by Pat Booth and Yvonne Martin in the *Eastern Courier* newspaper, which posed the central question: 'What lies behind the image of crowds of Asian children coming out of the best schools, the buy-up of expensive homes, slow erratic drivers in big new Mercedes and migration figures suggesting that Auckland is becoming the Taipei/Hong Kong/Seoul of the South Pacific?'

A decade later when Lydia and her family arrived 'it was a welcoming community in two senses,' says Spoonley. 'One was policy settings and the other was that the Korean community had become well-established and affluent. Lydia arrived here past the worst of the racism.'

In addition, the golf environment was ideal for her. Memberships among traditional golf devotees — older white men — were on the wane and clubs realised that they had to embrace the growing numbers of Asian citizens as well as offer more junior development if they were going to survive.

Critical to Lydia's development in this new setting was the merging of cultures. She is a classic example of 'generation 1.5', a name given to children of migrants who are born in one country but are educated in another. In many ways they arrive with the push of traditional values behind and are pulled into a new cultural setting through friends and school.

When Gil Hong and Tina arrived in Auckland, along with their bags they brought the Korean values and cultural principles they had grown up with — young Lydia would have been indulged until six or seven years old, when strict social training began. She would have learned to respect and obey her parents, who in turn would offer everything they could to help her achieve her dreams.

That traditional Korean parenting model applies to both education and pursuits such as golf. It ensured that once Lydia started learning the game her parents would be behind her 100 per cent, doing everything they could to smooth her chosen path. In return, she carried the responsibility of being fully committed, working hard, following her parents' guidance and making sacrifices that would justify the time and money invested in her.

'Children feel responsibility for their parents — that's the simplest way to put it,' says Wellington academic Jay Waters. 'You learn from a young age to respect your parents — your parents are scary.'

Young Lydia would have learned to respect and obey her parents, who in turn would offer everything they could to help her achieve her dreams.

Waters, a postgraduate research student at Victoria University of Wellington in the School of Languages and Cultures, has a particular interested in how sport, and golf especially, helps Korea's generation 1.5 children adapt to their new culture.

In coming to New Zealand for the sake of Lydia's golf, Gil Hong and Tina made sure to squeeze every drop of potential out of their daughter.

'Korean parents will push their children,' Waters says, 'and when we say "push" we mean support and encourage. The average Korean parent definitely has more influence on their children than western parents — directly and indirectly.'

On the other side of the equation to the strong, traditional Korean values was a Kiwi outlook that was more laidback.

As a result, transplanting Lydia from Korea to New Zealand just as she was starting school brought with it a drastic change in lifestyle. Instead of being in a Korean education system that can consume a child's entire day, Lydia jumped into a system offering plenty of time to practise golf without sacrificing a typical Kiwi education. In New Zealand it was possible to devote as much time to golf as to school.

What Lydia left behind when she had her passport stamped at Auckland International Airport is beyond the comprehension of Kiwi families. Schooling in Korea is incredibly competitive. In a credential-based society success is marked by results in high-pressure exams, and children spend most of their lives in some form of classroom. Waters, who lived for a number of years in Korea, describes it as a 'rat race'.

Gil Hong and Tina, both teachers, were well aware of what awaited their youngest daughter in the education system if they stayed in Korea. Escaping the 'rat race' to come to New Zealand, however, didn't remove their desire for her to succeed. Education remained vitally important, but instead of night schools and academies, the Ko family dedicated their non-school time to Lydia's golf.

Instead of private tutors to improve her maths and English, they invested in golf lessons. To be a teacher of any kind in Korea is to hold a highly regarded position in society. Teachers are greatly valued, and parents, recognising their own limitations, will always call in an expert — especially for a technical sport like golf.

'What separates Korea from New Zealand is Korean people will tend to ask for a teacher or professional coach, more than a Kiwi will,' says Waters. 'Parents are prepared to invest big-time in their children at a very young age.'

At first, Gil Hong took his daughter to the Takapuna driving range. Daniel Park, an employee there, has recalled Lydia's early days at the often crowded range. 'It was amazing,' Park said. 'Even then you could see the desire in her. She worked very hard; her whole family did. Especially her daddy.'

If Lydia had been born to Kiwi parents, the unknown factor is whether they would have sought out and invested as much as they did in coaching. If she'd stayed in Korea, the question is whether she would have found quite as much time for golf — or had access to facilities as good as those on offer to her in New Zealand.

As Korean parents, Tina and Gil Hong were committed to giving Lydia every chance to succeed. They could take their daughter to a golf course rather than a driving range and they could find a coach who was able to dedicate time and energy to her development.

Which is how Lydia ended up walking into Pupuke Golf Club, close to the Ko home on Auckland's North Shore, and meeting a fledgling golf coach by the name of Guy Wilson.

Chapter Three
A Guy and a girl

Guy Wilson was sitting in the pro shop at Pupuke Golf Club when Lydia Ko came skipping through the door with her mother in 2003. From behind his desk he could barely see the tiny child, so when Tina said she wanted lessons for her daughter he almost said no — figuring she was too small.

'She was so tiny I couldn't see her over the counter. She didn't speak much English and her clubs were all too big. Her driver was taller than her,' Wilson has recalled.

If he hadn't been 22 years old and starting out on his coaching career, he might have told the mother and daughter to go away and come back when Lydia was a bit bigger. But clients hadn't been banging down the door of the newly minted teaching professional, so when Tina wanted three half-hour lessons a week for Lydia, Wilson obliged.

He may well have wondered how on earth it would work. A young pro who didn't speak Korean and a young Ko still learning English — how hard would it be for the pair to communicate about the intricacies of swinging a golf club?

The trick, he quickly worked out, was to not worry about golf. Instead he would invent games to play with his pint-sized charge that instilled in her the basics of golf — putting and chipping — the elements critical to getting the ball in the hole in the fewest possible strokes. Taking account of her age and limited concentration span as well as the fact her equipment was much too big for her, he focused on the parts of the game that were the easiest to get right. And he did it by using a variety of props such as cones, hoops and different-coloured golf balls to create games that were fun as opposed to cranking out a succession of shots against the dull backdrop of a driving range.

A decade-long relationship blossomed on the fairways of Pupuke as Wilson became Lydia's coach, mentor, caddy and friend. Even though the partnership ended somewhat controversially just after she announced she was turning professional, Wilson will be forever remembered as the coach who made Lydia Ko, and he did it by appealing to the child in her.

The pair became a regular sight at Pupuke Golf Club, racing around in a golf cart, laughing and joking and developing a big brother–little sister–golf buddy relationship.

Despite their age difference, they enjoyed a laugh.

'Guy has a great sense of humour,' says David Niethe, who would become Lydia's mental trainer, 'and Lydia had her dad's cheeky sense of humour; they just clicked.'

Andrew Leventis, North Harbour Golf's executive officer, agrees: 'Guy was pretty light-hearted and kept the game fun for her at a young age. All the accolades for Guy are so deserved.'

Wilson also focused on what Lydia could achieve and in doing so helped build a key element of her game — an unerring accuracy in and around the green.

Too small and with clubs so big she could barely hit the ball more than 50 metres, Lydia was tasked with practising what golfers call the 'short game' — the little chips and pitches around the green that many amateurs ignore at their peril as they seek pleasure from blasting a ball into orbit with their driver.

Wilson believed Lydia could work on her distance when older and stronger, and that groundwork with the 'scoring clubs' — wedges and putter — is evident in the way Lydia plays the game more than a decade later.

On the LPGA Tour, Lydia's genius with chipping, pitching and other short-range shots such as from bunkers is obvious. She's the best putter on the tour, is one of the best in what they call 'sand saves' — recovering after hitting the ball into a bunker — and is in the top 10 for 'greens in regulation', which is a measure of her accuracy from the fairway.

In golf, these are the money shots and Wilson ingrained them in Lydia from a young age. These early lessons in short shots are in contrast to accepted golf teaching over the years. There's an old saying which various players have trotted out over time to simplify what they do: 'Hit the ball, find it, hit it again' — an implication that distance, rather than control, is the preferred way to play the game.

This is seen as a valid teaching method: teach the student to hit the ball with the required oomph and worry later about controlling its whereabouts. It's a method Wilson eschewed with his tiny protégée. In fact, he discouraged her from creating power because he worried her small, lean frame would be wrecked by the forceful twisting and torque required to muster distance.

John Lister, one of New Zealand's pioneering professional golfers, who would later have a leading hand in Lydia's development, well remembers seeing her in those early days, aged around seven, when her 'rubber-band' body spun and stretched through the golf swing. Wilson didn't want the rubber band to break, figuring a young golfer with tons of talent but a bad back wasn't going to win too many tournaments. For her long-range shots, he focused instead on creating an easy, flowing rhythm that didn't tax the body.

Nor did Wilson clutter Lydia's mind with redundant information about the almost-impossible-to-understand bio-mechanical principles of the golf swing.

Pam Greenhalgh, development manager at North Harbour Golf, who was in charge of representative teams featuring Lydia, says Wilson's methods worked a treat as Lydia learned the mechanics of the golf swing before understanding them. 'Guy pushed teaching games for understanding so he wasn't actually talking to her about swing mechanics. He was just playing a whole lot of games which were improving her swing without her really knowing.'

At the Ellerslie office of sports production company Sports Inc there is an old videotape with the words 'Do not erase — ever' written on the case.

Inside is a video recording of Lydia Ko, aged eight, and Guy Wilson at work, filmed at the Pupuke Golf Club in 2005.

In fact, there are two videos. On the first one, the tape is rolling for only a matter of seconds before the tiny child, dressed head to toe in pale pink, makes an effortless chip from the greenside rough. The ball pops gently into the air and rolls into the hole.

The cameraman, who had been sent down by Sports Inc boss

Phillip Leishman to determine if there was any truth to the hype surrounding this youngster, had switched on his camera just in time. Leishman took one look at it and sent a crew straight back to do a proper story.

Leishman, the face of golf broadcasting in New Zealand, passed away in February 2013, but his decision to document Lydia is a testament to his vision and to Wilson's belief in his unproven pupil — given that he was the one who suggested Sports Inc take a look at his girl wonder.

On the second video, which is closely guarded, Lydia is seen skipping down the fairway, doing cartwheels, diligently filling out her scorecard, joking with Wilson, laughing at herself, swinging with an effortless grace, and holing putt after putt for the camera.

Later Lydia is interviewed as she sits cross-legged on the grass. She speaks good English but not all her answers are clearly decipherable.

Asked why she started playing golf, she says: 'Dad said I have to play golf,' adding it was a choice of golf or ballet.

How did she get so good at golf? 'I didn't know how not to play golf.'

What does she love about golf? 'I don't know . . . chipping,' she says, rotating her upper body in a mime of the chipping movement.

When does she want to turn pro? 'At Guy's age.'

How old is Guy? 'I don't know.'

Asked to name her golf heroes, she thinks for a moment, points her finger at the reporter and says with total conviction: 'Annika Sörenstam!', referring to Sweden's 10-time major champion, before adding, 'Tiger Woods, Vijay Singh.'

At this stage in her young career, she has played against — and beaten — adults. How does she feel when she beats grown-ups? 'I be sorry for them.'

The reporter turns the discussion back to her parents and Lydia tells the camera her 'dad sometimes gets angry at me . . . if I hit it bad'. She then reveals her goal in life is to make an eagle — and we learn her mother has provided the incentive. 'If I do an eagle I will get a hundred dollars.'

She also shows an acute awareness of how fickle the game of golf can be, saying that, despite all her practice, 'the ball goes where it wants to'.

On the same video, Guy Wilson revealed that Lydia was now one of 60 or 70 young children he coached, ranging in age from five to twelve. They all practise hard, he says, 'but no one is as relentless as Lydia'. And despite Lydia's assertion the ball goes where it wants, Wilson is adamant 'she hits it in the exact same place all the time'.

Wilson had been coaching Lydia for two years at that point and although he might not have identified her potential on first meeting — hardly surprising given she was a tiny six-year-old — it didn't take long before he 'figured she had something special'.

But while Wilson had a huge impact on teaching Lydia the basics of golf, her father Gil Hong had a much stronger hand in his daughter's early development than has previously been credited.

Many believe Gil Hong and Tina handed over their daughter to Wilson, but it is clear from the start they formed a team. Gil Hong, with his qualification as a physical education teacher, intimately plotted his daughter's talent development. He just managed to do so while staying anonymously in the background. 'Her dad is the number one influence in her whole development — and still is,' says an insider familiar with the family.

But forget all those thoughts of overbearing fathers whipping their children towards a future retirement scheme. Gil Hong Ko, say those who know him well, is not your stereotypical driven father, even though Wilson once described him as having 'the Korean mindset, that hours and hours of practice will get the results, which has been proven'.

From the start Wilson and Lydia's parents worked in unison, navigating their way around any language barriers, and ensuring Lydia's best interests were at the centre of every decision they made. Importantly, Gil Hong and Guy Wilson shared the view that creating a fun and varied environment for Lydia was the best approach.

Gil Hong believed in a commitment to practice, but he rejected the accepted theory that success could only be built on mind-numbing repetition. He put enjoyment and fun at the heart of everything he did with Lydia and was committed to creating a constantly changing environment that stimulated his young daughter and preserved her interest in the game.

Starting early in any endeavour, whether it's writing software or hitting golf balls, is these days regarded as essential for creating champions. The quintessential example in golf is Tiger Woods, who famously made his first television appearance on the US *Mike Douglas Show* as a toddler. Rory McIlroy is another golfer famously filmed chipping balls into his mother's washing machine when still a boy.

When Tiger started out almost 40 years ago they didn't have a description for the journey ahead of him — though the old saying 'practice makes perfect' comes to mind — but now we do: '10,000 hours' is the catchphrase popularised by writer Malcolm Gladwell in his 2008 book *Outliers: The Story of Success*.

Gladwell didn't invent the 10,000 hours theory, but in investigating the research of psychologist K Anders Ericsson he observed a key factor separating the greats from the not-so-greats, pointing out a commonality among high achievers: they all engaged in 'deliberate practice' for a minimum of 10,000 hours. Whether it was Microsoft's Bill Gates in front of a clunky computer, a virtuoso violinist, or The Beatles bashing out music into the early hours of the morning at Berlin clubs, Gladwell's focus on the time they'd put in has made '10,000 hours' one of the most overused phrases in sport in recent years.

Gil Hong, through his background in physical education and the fact he played tennis to a high level, knew a lot about athletic development. But he also filtered his knowledge through his own personality and outlook. Those who know him say he's easy-going, light-hearted, jovial and enjoys a drink.

To become a great athlete, Gil Hong believed, required versatility, adaptability and creativity; he considered these qualities more important than 10,000 hours — or any number of robotic repetitions. He believed in stretching his daughter with challenges that became critical to her development path, but not in the manner of Se Ri Pak being forced to sit alone in a graveyard at night.

It wasn't enough to practise shots from the unchanging, forgiving surface of a driving range mat; Gil Hong would have Lydia practising in a variety of ways, including off slopes, on different surfaces and from varying positions. In that regard Pupuke Golf Club — cut into a steep hillside overlooking the Hauraki Gulf in Auckland's Campbells Bay — was an ideal physical environment. It taught Lydia how to play a myriad of different shots from ever-changing angles and slopes.

Journalist Simon Plumb was a young sports reporter on the *North Shore Times* and an avid golfer when Lydia first burst into prominence. In those early years he spent a lot of time watching her practise and came to understand some of the techniques Gil Hong employed.

'At the practice green, her dad would set up balls, maybe four or five balls in one spot, then he'd move around the green, drop four or five more, then another four or five, and she'd follow him — chip, chip, chip — and that could go on all day.'

K Anders Ericsson, the academic who first proposed the 10,000 hours theory, copped some criticism when Gladwell's book *Outliers* was published, mainly because Gladwell had turned scientific research into pop psychology but also because people misunderstood the original research.

In response, Ericsson revisited the subject in 2013, answering his critics. The density of the research makes it impossible to summarise, but it lends credence to the path Gil Hong had mapped out for Lydia. At one point Ericsson wrote: 'Nobody becomes an Olympic level gymnast or world class musician by simply doing more of the same simple activity that they started out doing as a beginner. In sum, engagement in particular training activities is necessary to create new adaptations at different levels of performance.'

Lydia's golf hours were tightly focused, but the heart of her routine was not mindless repetition. Gregg Thorpe, the high performance manager for New Zealand Golf, the sport's governing body, believes this approach was critical to her development. 'Guy and her dad were very good at getting the most out of her time. It was never about hitting ball after ball. It was about challenging her and her decision making and playing the game, not just ingraining techniques.'

The meshing of Gil Hong's theories about fun and variety and Wilson's innately youthful attitude towards coaching his young charge proved a blessing for Lydia, and offered a key to

It was never about hitting ball after ball. It was about challenging her and her decision making and playing the game, not just ingraining techniques.

her early development.

Simon Plumb believes Guy Wilson's personality was an important influence on Lydia. 'You'd see them at the range at Gulf Harbour and they'd be joking around, having a laugh,' he says. 'I think he's had a great influence on how she carries herself on a golf course and the way she doesn't get too wound up — he just lightened everything all the time. To his credit he probably saw you couldn't be too intense with someone that young.'

The creative, amusing, varied, pressure-free, easy-going environment created by Gil Hong and Guy Wilson perfectly matched Lydia's fun-loving personality, something that is still evident today.

Lydia's childhood mental trainer David Niethe believes she had a high level of self-awareness and understood from a young age what worked best for her. It was that attitude that made a rather difficult game approachable in the early years.

But it's one thing to make training and practice fun when there's nothing at stake. Taking the training mindset to the competitive field demands something else of a player.

Pam Greenhalgh managed the North Harbour team when Lydia was first picked to play at a senior level, at the ripe old age of 10. In interprovincial team golf, players are ranked in their team from No. 1 down to No. 5 and play matches against similarly ranked opponents from rival teams. At Lydia's first interprovincial tournament, in Nelson, she played as a No. 5 — the bottom-ranked player in the North Harbour team.

'She could have played higher,' says Greenhalgh. 'She was good enough, but because it was her first time in senior golf and she was only ten we decided to ease her in.

'I vividly remember that tournament because you'd see her skipping down the fairway, not watching what her opponents were doing, picking daisies. She was just a fun kid and different to so many kids you see coming through. Lydia would win her games by a mile and just go back to watch cartoons.'

Everywhere Lydia went, mum Tina was there too, a silent presence on the fringes of the fairway, watchful but never interfering. She was on hand to look after her daughter, keep her supplied with her favourite foods and do her laundry, but otherwise she stayed in the background, entrusting others to run things as they saw fit.

Gil Hong shared that restrained approach. While his supervision of her practice focused on enjoyment and variety, the sessions were demanding and the hours long, and the challenges came thick and fast for his precocious daughter. And despite Lydia's on-camera claims aged eight that her dad sometimes got angry with her, no one familiar with the young Lydia remembers any external pressure, no evidence of the so-called Ugly Parent Syndrome, no finger-waving, no shouting . . . no behaviour of the kind that has forced sports organisations in New Zealand to form policies around just such negative parenting.

'Her parents are calm in nature, quite relaxed, there's no yelling on the course, which is in contrast to what we see from some parents,' says Greenhalgh. 'Some parents are very intense . . . Lydia's golf was not hugely structured in that regard.'

In this fashion, Lydia's parents were non-conformists when it came to the perceived role of how to be a golf parent; they were supportive and ever-present but not overbearing or aggressive.

That guidance at a distance, and just-right encouragement, allowed Lydia to play golf the way she practised it, taking the belief system of fun and enjoyment from the practice fairway onto the course and into tournaments.

Make no mistake, she was competitive and driven, but she didn't play with any external pressure; she was doing it for herself and if that meant she was going to skip down fairways or laugh and joke between shots, that's what she did.

Ryan Fox, the son of legendary All Black first five-eighth Grant Fox and New Zealand's No. 1 male amateur at the same time Lydia was dominating the women's amateur game, said Lydia 'always looked like she was having fun. She never put any pressure on herself to perform; she just loved being out there. She has a great sense of humour and she just takes that out on the golf course with her.'

It doesn't mean she didn't get the odd push from parents who perfectly complemented each other. Tina's introversion, guardedness and astute intelligence is balanced by Gil Hong's outgoing nature, boisterous sense of humour and laidback disposition. Lydia had a self-driven discipline that came from her mother, coupled with her dad's cheeky, easy-going quick-wittedness.

Other Korean-Kiwi families might look at the Ko clan and wonder what it is that sets them apart, what they do differently. After all, plenty of other girls of Lydia's generation have the skill and the work ethic backed by strong parental desire for success.

But how many parents would channel all their energy and time into the betterment of their child's golf? How many mothers would be there every step of the way? Tina certainly was, whether it was picking up Lydia at lunchtime from Pinehurst, a private school on Auckland's North Shore, to shuttle her to the driving range for a quick practice before heading back to classes, or travelling around the country to tournaments to take care of Lydia's every need.

The short answer is that no matter what others might have done, Gil Hong and Tina went further. They sacrificed everything for Lydia's golf.

'They were all-or-nothing support; it wasn't a half-hearted

commitment; there was no fall back, no what-if, no back-up plan,' says a Korean golf dad who knows the family. 'Kiwis say, "I'm taking my kid to soccer practice, rugby practice at the weekend" and they think that is commitment — this was a different level of commitment.'

Lydia, in dutiful Korean fashion, did her best to repay the parental support and sacrifice, recalling later in life: 'When I started at six, sometimes I wanted to go on the playground because the kids were playing on it but I didn't, I went to the driving range.'

Contained in that comment is a hint of a lost childhood, but those who know how Korean families work understand it in a different way; it was how she fulfilled her duty in trying to repay her parents. It was a sacrifice, but it was one for people she loved and therefore not a negative thing.

And, yes, if there was a moment when she wavered, there would be that Korean push — but never a shove.

In this way, the Ko family walked a very fine line between two cultures. In the style of all Korean parents, they gave support when needed, and in a more Kiwi way they stepped back and let Lydia find her own way, without abdicating all responsibility and leaving Lydia to decide when and where she was going to practise. Too firm and they would risk taking the fun out of things; too loose and they would risk losing everything they had invested.

That kind of guidance is not at odds with fun when seen through the Korean family dynamic, says Jay Waters.

'Kids still have fun — they just have fun in different ways. And from what I've read, Lydia was completely engaged and immersed in what she was doing so the challenge must have been matched to her level.

'What is important is that her parents can't have pushed

her that hard otherwise she couldn't have made it through the ranks like she has.'

Having fun stayed with Lydia as she evolved as a golfer — and stays with her still. It has become something of a mantra in her press conferences and media statements. Enjoyment, she keeps telling the world, is what it's all about.

All the same, it's easier to have fun and enjoy yourself when you're winning. But, early in Lydia's stellar career, winning didn't come as readily as many imagine.

Chapter Four

Challenging times

The public life of Lydia Ko began with a passing mention. The last line in a stock-standard report sent out via the now defunct New Zealand Press Association in March 2005 read: 'Lydia Ko, seven, the youngest player to contest the championship, shot 100.'

And, no, we we're not talking the under-10s championship, not even the under-21s, but the New Zealand Women's Stroke Play Championship — the pinnacle amateur event on the calendar, contested at one of the country's most prestigious courses, Titirangi, in West Auckland.

It's the only course in New Zealand designed by famed British architect Alister MacKenzie, who created the masterpiece of Augusta National in Georgia, the site of the annual Masters tournament, as well as Royal Melbourne, regarded as the jewel in Australia's golfing crown.

On a good day, a grown man off a standard 18 handicap might be happy to go around Titirangi in 90 to 100 shots. With its tight fairways demanding accuracy, it also requires a variety of shots combined with the mental discipline to navigate the course the way MacKenzie intended. With its famously fast and subtly sloping greens (greens that can give you a heart attack, said one Kiwi professional) asking constant questions, Titirangi is a beautiful demon which can bite the most experienced players.

And a seven-year-old girl — a tiny one at that — shot an even 100, made to look even better by the fact the slope index for the course (a measure of its degree of difficulty) was 140 that week, comparable to the set-up for a professional event.

The fact little Lydia Ko even qualified to play in the tournament should have raised journalistic eyebrows. How did she get in the field? Where had she come from? Who taught her how to play? Is she the best seven-year-old in the country? What had Tiger Woods done when he was seven?

But the kid almost snuck under the radar.

A week later, David Leggat, in an article about the flourishing youth of the local golf scene, wrote in the *New Zealand Herald*:

'This is a true story: during last week's women's national amateur championships, the field included a seven-year-old.

'Lydia Ko of the Pupuke club shot a 98 and three rounds of 100 or just over off a 14 handicap. Onlookers reported that, like most seven-year-old girls, she skipped down the Titirangi fairways.'

Leggat noted: 'The field also included 10-year-old Cecilia

Choi, of Whitford Park, 11-year-old Katie Seo, three 13-year-olds and eight 14-year-olds.'

The fact is, Lydia Ko had no right to even be in the contest.

Within a year of having Lydia under his watchful eye, Guy Wilson thought he had something special on his hands.

And Gil Hong Ko believed in challenging his daughter, pushing the boundaries of what she could achieve. Neither coach nor father wanted to limit Lydia's horizons by restricting her to just practice rounds, no matter how varied; they wanted to test her in a competitive environment, to play golf rather than practice shots.

By having a golf-club membership, Lydia could get a handicap, which immediately gave her a benchmark against which she could measure herself. She could gauge improvement and Wilson would know whether their practice regime produced results.

A handicap also allowed her to enter competitions, to play against others in tournaments. And her parents wanted her to keep testing herself, said one insider.

'They've always taken the hard road. When they thought she was good enough to play there was no thought of holding her back — they never thought she was too young, or that school should come first.'

The problem, however, was Lydia's age. At seven, a golf-club membership at Pupuke was officially still three years away, as the club rules restricted junior memberships to children 10 and over. But Guy Wilson, with the backing of the Ko family, decided his young charge was mature enough to warrant a membership and lobbied the club for a dispensation.

The club rejected Wilson's first pitch, but he kept knocking on the door until they conceded — a key moment in unleashing the juggernaut Lydia Ko would become. As a paid-up member of Pupuke, for a fee of around $100, Lydia got a New Zealand Golf handicap. It was such a bargain she talks about it to this day in press conferences when she's asked the benefits of having grown up playing golf in New Zealand as opposed to Korea.

Her first recorded round of golf as a member, on Sunday, 12 December 2004, was a score of 89 off the yellow (junior) tees at Pupuke. A week later she shot 95. Two days later she ventured to the rugged and steeply undulating Waitakere Golf Club, situated within a regional park in the Waitakere Ranges. It's a daunting challenge for many just to walk the entire 18 holes of this demanding track. But Lydia took it in her little stride, carding a mightily respectable 84.

Another round, on Christmas Eve, at Pupuke delivered an 89 and when Lydia carded 88 at Pupuke on 28 December she had completed the minimum five rounds to earn her first handicap: 12.8. Some golfers might play their entire lives hoping to get a handicap as low.

Fourteen rounds of golf in January before presumably going back to school in February brought her handicap down to 11.3, good enough to earn her a start in the New Zealand Women's Stroke Play Championship at Titirangi on 11–14 March.

Aged seven, but six weeks shy of her eighth birthday, Lydia had somehow arrived at the pinnacle of amateur golf in New Zealand within three months of getting a handicap. And it wasn't to everyone's liking.

Peter Williams, the TVNZ broadcaster, talented golfer and former board member of New Zealand Golf, spoke for the critics in his *Herald on Sunday* column, saying Lydia's appearance against the best amateur players in New Zealand and Australia was 'extraordinary' — but not in a good way.

'Her best round at the relatively easy Takapuna public course is 80, in itself a remarkable number for one so young. But at Titirangi her four rounds were 100, 106, 98 and 111 — she came last. The woman marking her card for the final round told me she had a running battle with Lydia's father, her caddy, to ensure Lydia's correct score was entered on each hole.'

He added: 'She appeared to not know important and basic rules, such as not being allowed to ground a club in a hazard.'

Williams then detailed the now famous story of Lydia's inability to hit the ball across the bush-clad gully on the 15th hole. After trying a few times to hit the ball the required 150 metres to reach land on the opposite side, Lydia eventually chipped the ball towards the edge of the gully, a shot of some 40 or 50 metres, in order to give herself a chance to keep playing the hole. As it was a strokeplay competition, she had to record each shot, and it's little wonder there was some confusion over her score, given how many balls ended up in the gully.

Williams was adamant she should not have been allowed to play despite her handicap being good enough to warrant entry.

'It would seem it wasn't Lydia's fault that she was entered but her parents'. . . . The influx of Korean youth into New Zealand golf has seen a marked increase in the number of ambitious parents offering every possible support to their child, often to a point that borders on the ridiculous.'

Williams then detailed the type of behaviour many Kiwis associated with pushy Asian parents: a 10-year-old practising in the rain by the light of car headlights, a youngster not allowed to go to bed until she'd made 100 putts, children being 'beaten' for not playing well.

'The issue is important because so many future New Zealand champions and national representatives will be Korean.' Williams thought, however, that golf would play an important role in assimilating Koreans and other Asian groups into New

Zealand society. 'I regularly see teenagers, who have been in this country for a few years, mixing with other junior golfers of other ethnic backgrounds. But,' he noted, 'the hopes of their parents' generation regularly cause tension.'

Williams' strong comments concluded with a demand for Women's Golf New Zealand to put an age limit on such events to stop parents driving their children too hard.

If Lydia had disappeared, never to be seen again because Titirangi had brutalised her or she'd been whipped too hard, too soon, she would have been chalked up as just another promising kid with a career ruined by overbearing parents.

But — and it's easy to say in hindsight — this seven-year-old was different. She wasn't going away. In fact, it was just this kind of challenge that inspired her to try harder.

Within a few months the quibbling over whether a seven-year-old, no matter how talented, was being pushed too hard by her immigrant parents faded into the background of the golf landscape. By June 2005 people were talking about only one New Zealand golfer, after Michael Campbell claimed the 2005 US Open.

Through a quirky coincidence Campbell won his major title, only the second for New Zealand after Bob Charles' 1963 British Open win, by holding off a charging Tiger Woods at a golf cathedral known as Pinehurst No. 2 in South Carolina. Lydia Ko, at the time, attended Pinehurst School on Auckland's North Shore.

With all the media fuss around Cambo, another year passed before Lydia's name graced the papers again, this time in the *Waikato Times* wrap-up of the New Zealand age-group golf championships in Morrinsville, where she was described as the 'remarkable Pupuke nine-year-old' after winning the under-13 age-group title.

A year later she finished ninth in the national amateur strokeplay championship in Taranaki. Still just 10 years of age, she was now a genuine talent on the national scene.

Her first golfing trip overseas, in 2007, took her to the Callaway Junior World Championship, played over three rounds at a par-three course in Santa Fe, New Mexico. She finished two strokes out of the lead as runner-up in the 9-to-10-year-old girls' division.

A year later she finished ninth in the national amateur strokeplay championship in Taranaki, shooting three consecutive rounds of 78, a far cry from that last-place finish and scores of around 100 at Titirangi. Still just 10 years of age, she was now a genuine talent on the national scene.

In October 2008, North Harbour named her in the five-person team to contest the interprovincial championships in Nelson, the biggest event on the New Zealand women's golf calendar. North Harbour narrowly missed qualifying for the semi-finals, but the *Nelson Mail*'s coverage of the event identified Lydia as the 'bright light' of the tournament.

The bubbling news around Lydia drove *North Shore Times* reporter Simon Plumb to seek out this promising talent to see whether the fuss was justified. He bravely went head to head with a girl half his age and half his height, playing a nine-hole match at the North Shore Golf Club.

'I honestly don't know how she got so good. I met her when she was eleven and she was already class,' Plumb recalls.

'After that nine holes when she'd beaten me — and I was a little punch-drunk to be honest, wondering "how am I going to tell my mates I got beaten by an eleven-year-old girl?" — she went to the practice bunker to work some more on her game.'

Plumb went over to watch; he wanted to see more.

'In the bunker she was hitting sand wedges with absolute consistency — they were all settling within two or three feet of each other — and at that point I realised she wasn't just a good, talented youngster. I don't know how many adult professionals could do that — she really had something.'

More than the golf, Plumb vividly recalls the young girl's surprising maturity. What she lacked in physical stature, she made up for with force of personality.

'There was no awkwardness with her. From the get-go Lydia was just fun, and really open. I would try to interview her as we were walking down the fairway and she'd answer the question but then come back at me with a question of her own. Just stuff like, "What's your favourite movie?" And then we'd be talking about *Kung Fu Panda*. Just sweet stuff.'

Plumb met Lydia over the years at Gulf Harbour, where he was a member.

'Most athletes in that environment would not want a bar of it if they saw a journalist in that environment, but she'd cruise over and ask how my game was going and I remember thinking, "You're a genuine person." She had old-school values.'

In April 2016 Plumb met Lydia for the first time in two years at Augusta.

'She sees me, says "hey" and comes straight over. In our work you meet a lot of athletes and politicians who have a sense of plastic about the interaction you have with them. I put Lydia in the same class as Val Adams, the double Olympic gold medal shotputter — open, honest and true about what she means.'

Around six weeks after Plumb's revelatory loss to Lydia she reached a landmark in her short career. On 1 January 2009, her New Year's Day round of 73 at Pupuke — one of nine consecutive scores of 73 at Pupuke over nine straight days during the holiday period — dropped her handicap officially to 0.0 or, as they say in the trade, scratch.

To answer Simon Plumb's question on how Lydia had become so good at such a young age, well, she'd been working damn hard for four years and had access to some of the best minds in golf.

In looking back on those early years, Guy Wilson has acknowledged the graft his student put in — he has been quoted as saying 'Lydia hits more golf balls than anyone. She just doesn't get fazed. She just keeps beating balls, beating balls, beating balls, working on it every day' — and the equally committed effort from the family, which, he has noted, was much more than many Kiwi children and their families put in.

'The difference is the Koreans are happy to invest in it. They will spend money on it, do it properly, get the coaching. They aren't like the average Kiwi kid whose parents buy some clubs and say, "Go and play golf."'

Lydia's lessons from her father and Wilson got positive reinforcement in these early years from two of New Zealand's most respected professionals, John Lister and Bob McDonald.

At the time, McDonald coached New Zealand representative Sharon Ahn, who has since left New Zealand to go back to Korea where she has reverted to her Korean name, Shin Ae Ahn. These days she is better known for her glam looks and hanging out with Korean celebrities, though her golf game remains in good order.

She and Lydia crossed paths in that ground-breaking tournament in Titirangi in 2005 where seven-year-old Lydia finished last. Sharon, at 14, finished at the other end of the field, winning the tournament.

Sharon's parents Anthony and Rosemary ran the cafeteria at the Takapuna driving range, where Sharon hit balls under the watchful gaze of McDonald and her father. In the close-knit North Shore Korean golf community, Lydia's parents naturally crossed paths with Sharon's and a bond was formed which resulted in Lydia and Sharon playing practice rounds together.

Sharon's regular Sunday routine was an early morning tee-off at Gulf Harbour on the Whangaparaoa Peninsula north of Auckland, with her coach McDonald and his old mate Lister.

Soon, Lydia joined the group, with Tina riding shotgun on the edge of the fairway with bags of sushi rolls at the ready for her daughter. Lister estimates he played 20 practice rounds a year with Lydia when she was between the ages of eight and 12.

Those Sunday mornings were integral to Lydia's development as a player, but they also served as a motivation. Sharon, as the youngest winner of the national title, became a natural measuring stick for Lydia.

'By the time Sharon got to sixteen and Lydia was ten, Sharon could see Lydia was catching up quick,' Lister says. 'The goal for Lydia was right there in front of her.'

Lister is a big man and in the 1970s he was a big talent, dominating the New Zealand professional circuit and winning the 1976 Quad Cities Classic on the PGA Tour in the United States.

He's also irreverent and outspoken but he knows the game of golf inside out and he's a firm believer in two things: enjoying yourself and actually 'playing' the game, which means creating shots to suit circumstances rather than playing every shot as if set up on a driving range. Again, this fitted in with Gil Hong's theory that Lydia needed to be creative and versatile.

Lydia learned the art of course management — the best way to navigate a golf course — as much by osmosis as by any direct teaching as she watched two experienced professionals plot their way around the tough Gulf Harbour layout.

She learned that it was sometimes better to aim to the left or right of a fairway, rather than straight down the middle, to create better angles towards the hole location. She also came to understand that a straight ball flight was not always the best option as some holes favoured a ball flight that curved left to right (a fade) while others demanded a right to left shape (a draw).

Lister downplays his input as just a gentle nudge here or a suggestion there. In his mind, educating Lydia required little effort as she had an appetite for learning which matched her appetite for food. ('Lydia had the biggest appetite of any girl I've seen; she was like a vacuum hoovering it down. She would down these huge hamburgers in a flash.')

In John Lister's opinion, 'Lydia was born to play golf. She just understood the game better than other people.

'There are professionals I've tried to help who still don't understand what she does and they are forty years old. I've seen Korean players with better swings than Lydia — and lots of people who try to perfect their swings but what they need to do is perfect their shots. No two shots are the same, and Lydia understood that. And she realised the game wasn't about hitting spectacular shots, but about eliminating mistakes.

'When the nitty-gritty comes Lydia wins because she doesn't make any errors.'

During this period, Lydia started to collect headlines for all the right reasons as she carved a path on the national golf scene.

Her first big breakthrough came at the North Island Stroke-play Championship at Muriwai Golf Club, on the rugged west coast of Auckland. The wind-lashed course offers a compelling test of links golf, one which Lydia passed with ease in April 2009, just two weeks before her 12th birthday.

With rounds of 77-74-70-74, Lydia had to nail a 2 metre putt on Muriwai's testing three-tiered 18th green to win the title over another Korean-Kiwi, Hanee Song, who was a year older than Lydia and had herself been subject to press reports touting her as the next big thing.

Lydia admitted afterwards her hands were shaking as she lined up her victory putt — a long comeback putt for par — after she'd hit her birdie too hard. 'Because I had a long putt to win the tournament I was really nervous,' she said.

Lydia celebrated her 12th birthday two weeks later during the national amateur championship, which took her back to Titirangi where she'd first come to public attention five years earlier. Here she would start a career-defining rivalry with yet another young Korean-Kiwi.

Chapter Five

The Ko and Cho Show

When they decided to emigrate to New Zealand, the Ko family didn't have a grand plan to turn their golf-loving daughter into a world-beater.

But once she had gained a club membership and her handicap fell swiftly to scratch, it became clear she had the capability to achieve great things. A plan was needed, so Team Ko set their sights on her becoming the best amateur in the world, then to turn professional and become the best player on the planet.

According to a friend of the family, the plan mapped out Lydia's life for the following 30 years.

'Koreans are used to planning their children's careers maybe ten years ahead but Lydia's parents were thinking twenty and thirty years ahead — that's what is unique about Gil Hong and Tina; they knew how to architect and build her career from a very young age.

'The whole aspect of making Lydia world number one started very early and right from day one they had the vision, they knew where were they were going and they had no second thoughts.

'And they were different to many Koreans who focus on the physical play and hard practice — Lydia's parents knew she had to learn how to work with media, how to articulate herself. They understood the mental aspect, the stretching, the strength . . .'

That holistic outlook took them to the newly formed Institute of Golf in Albany, Auckland, established by golf coach Craig Dixon, mental trainer David Niethe and physiotherapist Brad Takai. The institute is a one-stop shop for golfers, providing a small driving range and state-of-the-art indoor technology to record swing data. A physical trainer, mental coach and physiotherapist were all on hand to provide Lydia with everything she needed to improve all facets of her game.

Guy Wilson, who is now a shareholder in the business alongside Dixon and Niethe, was one of the founding coaches.

The family's laser-etched plan for their budding star also required her to get noticed. To make the necessary impression that would open doors on the world stage, Lydia had to win tournaments such as the New Zealand Amateur Championship and the Australian Amateur Championship. This would lead to other tournaments, most importantly, the US Amateur Championship, a competition that has launched dozens of stars in the United States through the widespread media coverage it gets from all outlets, from news agencies to glossy magazines.

Lydia had started her journey years younger than many others, thanks to Guy Wilson's canny lobbying for an early membership at Pupuke. This meant anything Lydia achieved would invariably be prefaced with 'youngest ever . . .'

Such was the case in late April 2009, when the just-turned-12 Lydia reached the final of the New Zealand Amateur Championship at Titirangi — and not just any final but one featuring the youngest combatants in the event's 115-year history: Lydia Ko, 12, versus Cecilia Cho, 14.

Cho versus Ko — it was the start of a rivalry that would define both young Korean imports.

Until that point, despite their talents, the two girls had not played against each other in competition, but Lydia knew exactly who her rival was, having watched Cecilia's blooming talent unfold.

'I know Cecilia well but we've never played against each other,' she said ahead of the 36-hole final, in which Lydia had the chance to become the youngest ever winner.

The hype and expectation in the golf community around the clash was somewhat muted by Cecilia delivering a consistently mistake-free performance to grind out a convincing win over a younger rival who made a handful of errors.

All the same, Lydia's performance in reaching the final, and giving herself a shot at history, turned plenty of heads. Guy Wilson was more convinced than ever his charge had a huge future, saying afterwards: 'The sky's the limit really for Lydia, as long as the interest remains and she can keep developing.'

What kept Lydia's interest in the immediate future was figuring out a way to beat her older rival as a series of clashes unfolded over the next three years.

Cecilia's rise to the top of the amateur New Zealand rankings was perfect for Lydia because Sharon Ahn, on whose back she'd previously set her sights, had returned to Korea. No sooner had Sharon gone than Cecilia was in the frame and Lydia had another target at which to aim.

'Lydia and Cecilia won everything,' says Pam Greenhalgh of North Harbour Golf, 'but Cecilia was a little bit older and won a lot before Lydia turned the tables. It was good for Lydia to have someone about the same age pushing her.'

Their rivalry heightened Lydia's desire to improve and find ways to beat Cho, who became equally a friend and a competitor. The fact Cecilia would soon be rated the No. 1 amateur player in the world also gave Lydia and her family reason to believe their plan for her could come to fruition. The pathway to the top of the world suddenly came into focus as both clearly visible and achievable.

Critical to Lydia's development is that she admired and respected Cecilia for what she'd accomplished; her older rival was an inspiration to improve her own game. There is a subtle but important difference between wanting to rise to someone else's level as opposed to conquering someone or taking them down.

Rather than stay like boxers in their opposite corners, the two girls bonded over music and TV shows: K-pop and Korean soap operas. They became friends who spurred each other to greater heights.

'That rivalry with Cecilia was quite important,' says David Niethe, who coached both players in mental-strength skills.

'Cecilia was different from Lydia to coach from a mental side of things. She was very intellectual — she would constantly question things. "Why" was a very strong word in her vocabulary; she would use it a lot — "Why is that?" she'd ask all the time, and you'd have to go into great depth to explain things.

'Lydia in contrast was like a sponge. They were quite different, but they were also extremely close friends . . . and very, very firm competitors, and in that regard I think Cecilia played a major role in Lydia's development. It conditioned both of them.'

The tug of war with Cecilia provided the perfect kind of talent-modifying stress Gil Hong was seeking for Lydia. But how would she respond to losing? Would it toughen her or wear her down?

A month after she missed a chance to become the youngest ever New Zealand amateur champion by losing to Cecilia, Lydia again found herself in her rival's wake, finishing runner-up to her in the Tauranga Open.

Another rival — and future national teammate — emerged that year in the form of Emily Perry, who at 18 was considerably older than Cecilia and Lydia. Like Sharon Ahn, Emily, from Waikato, was coached by Lydia's Sunday-morning playing partner, Bob McDonald.

Emily's first big win in September 2009, at the Wairakei Open in Taupo, came at the expense of a much younger Lydia. The pair were tied for the lead with nine holes to play, but a triple bogey by Lydia on the 15th hole dropped her back to an eventual third-placed finish.

Lydia turned the tables on Emily a few weeks later at the Taranaki Open at Ngamotu, blazing away to finish an incredible nine shots clear of her.

With Lydia in hot form, the North Harbour team headed to the interprovincial championships at The Grange in Auckland in October 2009. North Harbour picked Lydia, not yet a teenager, to play in the No. 1 spot.

Being No. 1 didn't necessarily make her the team leader, however.

'The leaders are the ones who have played a bit — the older teens,' says Pam Greenhalgh. 'As a twelve-year-old, even as good as she was, it would be tricky to sit down with older girls and say, "Hey, this is what I think." Even though she had the playing ability on the course, offering that leadership would have been a hard thing to do.

'And we didn't want to put her there anyway; we wanted her to focus on putting wins on the board.

'But I've never ever seen an arrogance or a cockiness from her — that's what made her really special. She just fitted in anywhere and let her scores do the talking. The rest of the time she's one of the girls. She realised she had talent but her personality is not to promote herself.'

All the same, the focus at the end of that interprovincial tournament fell firmly on Lydia, who went through the early stages unbeaten as she guided North Harbour into the final, where yet another showdown awaited with arch-rival Cecilia Cho, the Auckland No. 1.

The heartbreak and potential guilt that followed could have broken many young players.

With the match score in North Harbour's favour 2½ to 1½ after the players ranked No. 2 to No. 5 had finished their matches (North Harbour winning two, Auckland one, with one shared), Lydia and Cecilia were effectively duelling for the title.

Their individual match would determine their respective team's fate. For Lydia, it was simple. At worst she could share her match with Cecilia and North Harbour would win the coveted title 3-2.

In match play the overall score does not determine the outcome; rather, the players compete to win each hole. With each player shining — making six birdies apiece through 17 holes — they came to the last hole with the match all square.

Lydia had to match Cecilia shot for shot on the final hole and the title would be North Harbour's.

Both players took the same number of shots to get on the green and when Cecilia took two putts to make her par, Lydia knew she had two putts to halve the match and send her teammates into rapturous celebrations.

Her first putt finished less than a metre from the hole — an easy one to tidy up for such a talented young player. Tap it in, secure the half, enjoy the applause and the spray of champagne which her team manager had ready in anticipation of the team's victory.

But the putt missed. Lydia had lost the match. The overall scores were tied at 2½ to 2½ and the rules meant the respective No. 4s for each team would go out to play sudden death, with Auckland's Jesse Hamilton beating North Harbour's Faye-Amy Nickson to give Cecilia's Auckland team the title.

'It was really sad that day,' Lydia recalled. 'Our manager had the champagne ready to spray over us when we won but we ended up losing in the play-off so it wasn't too good.'

It may have been 'sad', but for Lydia there were no tears, no outward emotions, no beating herself up. In fact, those around her were almost shocked by the equanimity she showed.

'If that happened to me I'd be mortified,' says Andrew Leventis, North Harbour's executive officer. 'But her view was she did it, it happened, she wasn't trying to miss . . . she had an ability to get over the adversity and move on.'

'She just took it in her stride,' adds Pam Greenhalgh, who believes Lydia's youth insulated her from the consequences — and guilt — others would have felt at letting down their team.

'At that age you can be a little naive as to what's happening around you and not recognise consequences so much or worry about what other people are thinking. You're just a young person playing a sport and you don't see that other stuff.'

Despite the losses to Cecilia — who dominated New Zealand amateur golf in 2009, winning 15 titles — Lydia continued to catch the eye of writers and pundits, with words like 'genius' and 'prodigy' studding media reports, but the first journalist to see the future was *Waikato Times* reporter Ian Anderson, who wrote in October 2009:

'It's an outrageous thought — one of our leading contenders for gold at the 2016 Olympics will still be a teenager come Games time in Rio de Janeiro.

'It's a long shot — so much so that this week I started chasing bookmakers to offer me lucrative odds on Lydia Ko winning the women's golf gold medal at the 2016 Olympics.'

Anderson noted that Lydia 'is just 12 but has scary reserves of potential'.

Anderson's logic had only one flaw: Lydia couldn't yet call herself a New Zealander.

That status changed by the end of the year when she officially became a Kiwi after getting confirmation of her citizenship on Christmas Eve — 'such a great Christmas present', she said at the time. Getting citizenship under another flag is not taken lightly by Koreans as their country allows just one nationality, so to become a Kiwi she had to give up her Korean birthright.

She celebrated her new status by blitzing the field in the North Island Strokeplay Championship in Taupo by seven shots in January 2010, with Cecilia Cho a distant third.

At the end of the tournament, the newly minted New Zealander didn't hesitate to state her dream to represent her new country.

Within a month, New Zealand Golf had named Lydia to

make her senior debut alongside Cecilia Cho, 15, and 18-year-old Zoe Brake in the team that would contest the Queen Sirikit Cup, the top amateur women's event in the Asia-Pacific region.

Before then, Lydia had another step on the ladder to climb — competing against professionals in the New Zealand Open — and announcing herself to a wider, disbelieving audience.

The wind-buffeted Pegasus golf course in Christchurch is a major test for any player, let alone a 12-year-old playing in her newly adopted country's national open for the first time.

More than any other element, a strong breeze is a golfer's worst enemy. With the wind behind or in your face, it can make judging distance difficult, while cross-winds can send a ball sailing off course and into trouble. Controlling the flight of the ball in windy conditions is the bane of a golfer's life . . . unless you're Lydia Ko.

When a brisk northeasterly breeze turned to near gale force in the third round of the Open, it played havoc with the leaders on the difficult back nine, but Lydia withstood it superbly to play the back nine in par 36, for a one-under 71. She ended the 54 holes one under par for the tournament and tied for 11th.

Lydia came out in calmer conditions in the final round, shot a three-under-par 69 and finished in a tie for seventh place, winning the Bessie Fullerton-Smith Trophy for the leading amateur.

Experienced Englishwoman Laura Davies took the title and couldn't quite believe her eyes when she arrived for the prizegiving.

'I could see this little girl — she was a very small girl, too — and I was wondering "Who is this?" Then they were saying: "Leading amateur, Lydia Ko . . ." and up gets this tiny little thing and I thought, "Bloody hell, that's amazing."

'In my speech I said, "Congratulations Lydia, but it's six

'Honestly, I never thought in a million years I'd clap eyes on her again — she had these big glasses on, she was tiny, she didn't look like the future of golf, but we should have realised how good she was by what she shot.'

o'clock; shouldn't you be in bed by now?"

'Honestly, I never thought in a million years I'd clap eyes on her again — she had these big glasses on, she was tiny, she didn't look like the future of golf, but we should have realised how good she was by what she shot.'

As part of the Ladies European Tour (LET), the New Zealand Open attracted plenty of the world's best female golfers, many of whom realised they'd seen a budding star announce herself to a global audience.

Iben Tinning, of Denmark, described Lydia as 'being unbelievable already', while Norwegian Cecilie Lundgreen said 'it was incredible how a twelve-year-old seemed to be totally unfazed by everything that was going on around her'.

Lydia's press conference offered an insight into what made the youngster tick.

Going into the Open she had a goal to beat the benchmark set by — naturally — Cecilia Cho, who had won the leading amateur award the previous year by finishing in a tie for 14th. Lydia negotiated a reward with her mother: beat Cecilia's mark and she could get her ears pierced. This type of intra-family incentive scheme would continue to play a part in her career, even when she started to play for huge sums of money.

During the tournament Lydia struggled a little with her putting, but in the final round stroked the ball beautifully. Asked about the difference, she told media: 'My coach and caddy [Guy Wilson] recorded his voice saying "I love putting" and it helped me feel more comfortable.'

Incentives, support, mind games . . . those around her certainly knew how to get the best out of Lydia.

From the New Zealand Open, she had the rare blessing of making her senior international debut on home soil, with the Queen Sirikit Cup held at the Hamilton Golf Club in April

2010, where she was the youngest player in the field.

She batted away questions about her relative inexperience and dumbfounded reporters with her maturity when she said that her age didn't matter, that instead it was how many years she'd been playing. 'The longer you play you get more experience, so that's what you learn.'

New Zealand finished second to Korea in the tournament, but Lydia edged Cecilia Cho to finish as the top-ranked Kiwi.

Cecilia turned the tables in the next two head-to-head contests, winning the Ruth Middleton Memorial Tournament at Matamata by two shots from Lydia and then claiming the Taranaki Open, this time by eight shots from Lydia.

In October 2010, Lydia, Cecilia and Caroline Bon represented New Zealand in the pinnacle of women's amateur team golf — the Espirito Santo Trophy, the biennial amateur women's world championship, contested since 1964.

In a biography of players New Zealand Golf issued before the tournament, Lydia showed some of her personality when asked if she had any lucky charms or superstitions: 'Heart and star shapes. Pink, blue, purple and lime-green crystals! Rainbow-coloured ribbons. Yellow, lime green, light sky blue, purple, pink and white,' she replied exuberantly.

New Zealand finished a creditable eighth in the event, with Cecilia the leading individual in 16th place, shading Lydia by three shots. Team manager Libby Steele noted Lydia 'was outstanding in her first tournament at this level for such a young player'.

Lydia's 2010 ended with a redemptive performance.

A year after she missed that 1 metre putt to lose her critical match to Cecilia, handing the 2009 interprovincial title to arch-rivals Auckland, she and her North Harbour team ventured to the Miramar Golf Club in Wellington looking to go one better.

Lydia, unbeaten in eight matches and later named player of the tournament, found herself needing to halve her final match — this time against Waikato No. 1 Emily Perry — for North Harbour to win the tournament.

'They told me that I needed to get at least a half for us to win. I thought back to last year when it was the same and I didn't win but I blanked it out,' Lydia said at the time, before seeing off Emily with a confident victory.

Looking back, those formative years in which Ko and Cho went toe to toe throws up a raft of questions critical to both players' futures.

Is it better for a player's development to be the hunter rather than the hunted? Did the pursuit of an older rival provide the stimulus Lydia needed to keep pressing on after she reached the top? Did being cut down by a younger player have an adverse effect on Cecilia Cho?

As Lydia rose to No. 1 in the world, Cecilia, now known as Jeongmin Cho, battled away in relative anonymity, but not without success, on the Korean LPGA.

In March 2016 she won an event in Korea and her world ranking lifted to 82. She is also making plenty of money, though not as much as Lydia. Since turning professional she's earned in the realm of NZ$500,000 — about a tenth of what Lydia has earned but not bad at all.

Long-time golf observers struggle to identify why Lydia kept rising when Cecilia stalled. As children they both put in prodigious hours of practice: at least 40 hours a week; they had the same mental coach, the same access to facilities and coaches, and similar parental support.

Jeongmin's former coach Rory Moor even noted Cecilia,

as a teen, had a similar long-term plan to Lydia, stating in 2014 that 'her life for the next 10 years is planned out. It's not maybes, it's what she will do. What we [Kiwi] Caucasians say is, "Wouldn't it be nice if . . ." They [Koreans] say, "You are going to be a golf professional and not only that, you are going to be a very successful golf professional and this is how we are going to do it."'

Shortly before turning pro and leaving New Zealand, Cecilia confessed that being overtaken by her younger rival had taken an emotional toll: 'I think she [Lydia] deserves it. She worked for it. Sometimes it gets emotional but there's nothing I can do about it — except just work harder.'

Jeongmin Cho returns to New Zealand regularly and stays in touch with Lydia on Facebook and Instagram, and there's no doubt she's still working hard on her game — she is, after all, just two-and-a-half years older than Lydia and has plenty of time to claw her way back to the top. But whether the rivalry will be reignited in the future is, for now, a distant hope.

Chapter Six

Next big thing

In any listing of Lydia Ko's achievements the phrase 'became the youngest . . .' occurs numerous times.

What usually doesn't feature is the number of times she 'almost became the youngest . . .', as witnessed by her loss to Cecilia Cho when she strove to become New Zealand's youngest amateur champion. Things didn't necessarily go her way as she tried to rewrite history. The start of 2011 featured a similar scenario when she blew a chance to win the New South Wales Open, a professional event.

The Oatlands course, near Parramatta in western Sydney, finishes with a simple par-three hole of 114 metres.

Lydia stepped to the tee with a one-shot lead over Caroline Hedwall of Sweden. Literally all she had to do was a pitch and putt for a victory that would have made her — by quite some margin — the youngest player to win a women's professional golf tournament. She was 13, and three months shy of her 14th birthday.

And maybe there's a reason 13-year-olds don't win many professional golf tournaments: the pressure is intense. After Hedwall made a dramatic birdie under pressure at the 18th hole, Lydia, safely on the green, needed two putts to secure a place in a play-off. As in the dramatic interprovincial match against Cecilia Cho in 2009, she three-putted for a bogey four, missing her par putt from just under a metre. The two-shot swing in Caroline's favour handed the Swede victory. But just as she did when she blew it against Cecilia, Lydia didn't flinch at such a painful loss.

'The youngster smiled. She hadn't stopped smiling all day, but no tears were visible behind the large prescription glasses she wears,' wrote veteran golf journalist Peter Stone in the *Sydney Morning Herald.*

Lydia took the learning experience as just that, nothing more or less: 'I am disappointed that I missed that short putt, but I think when I have that kind of putt in my future tournaments I'll be more confident,' she said. 'I really want to take the positive out of it; it's a learning experience. The positives are good.'

Lydia went from the New South Wales Open back to Christchurch for another tilt at the New Zealand Open title, this time finishing fourth, again behind Laura Davies, and winning over the media with her charm and wit as she examined a less than satisfactory putting performance.

Reporter: What areas of your game are you working on?

Lydia: Putting, always putting.

Reporter: What's wrong with your putting?

Lydia: It's not going in.

Reporter: Why not?

Lydia: I don't know.

Reporter: The ball is not doing what it's told?

Lydia: Yeah. It's not my fault; it's the ball's. Or the hole is rejecting it.

There's an old golf adage, originally uttered by South African pro golfer Bobby Locke and made famous by Jack Nicklaus: 'Drive for show, putt for dough'. While not playing for cash as she was still an amateur, Lydia's putting definitely stopped her earning silverware. And she often three-putted — a cardinal sin in any golfer's book. The conventional way to make par on any golf hole is to take two putts on the green; a three-putt is like giving a shot back to the field.

Despite her unerring accuracy off the tee, Lydia struggled for a long time with her accuracy from close range on the greens.

Emily Perry, who would be a teammate of Lydia's at the Queen Sirikit Cup in India shortly after that New Zealand Open, is another to have benefited from Lydia's wayward putting in her early years.

'I once beat her in play-off — I was one of the only ones who did that because usually when she played she won everything,' Emily recalls. 'But that day was the worst I've ever seen her putt.'

Golfers who struggle with their putting can do so for a variety of reasons. Nerves can be a factor; their eyes might not be balanced; they might just have a bad technique.

Lydia's problems didn't seem to be nerves as she never seemed ruffled, and she won her first big event, the North Island Strokeplay Championship, despite shaking hands. And assuming her eyes were getting tested regularly and she had the right prescription in her trademark large glasses, it meant her putting woes were probably technical.

Like anything to do with technique, the answer is practice.

Despite her unerring accuracy off the tee, Lydia struggled for a long time with her accuracy from close range on the greens.

'Her putting problems weren't something that made her fearful,' says Emily Perry. 'She just went and worked at it until it became the best part of her game.

'She's like that with every part of her game. Where others would say, "This is too hard," or they work too hard on the wrong things, she says, "You know what? I'm going to work on *this*." And that's where the team around her are so good.'

Emily saw Lydia's work-ethic first hand in 2011 when the pair travelled the world as the nucleus of various New Zealand teams which also included Cecilia Cho. Lydia might have been the youngest player in the team, but Emily says Lydia was very professional and — as the best player — got to call the shots. In that regard, Lydia treated every event as if it was already her job. She was in a dress rehearsal for a future life where golf was going to be a living. While others hoped to make a success of a professional career, Lydia put in hours as if she already *was* a pro.

And Lydia's behaviour dictated the regime for the rest of the team. If she wanted to be at the practice range two hours before her tee time and stay two hours afterwards, the rest of the team did so as well.

'She was always practising and to be fair it improved all our games as we only had one minivan, so if Lydia wanted to practise the rest of us had to practise: the best player in the team called the shots and she was the best player,' recalls Emily.

But as soon as work was over, she flicked a switch and became a happy-go-lucky teenager with a wicked sense of humour. 'There were nights when we roomed together when we were crying with laughter at the silliest things,' Emily says.

It was tears of a different kind, however, at the Queen Sirikit Cup in Delhi, India, in late February when Lydia and her teammates suffered the ultimate test of their desire to play golf at the highest level.

On a diabolically constructed golf course cut out of the jungle, any tee shot that roamed even a short distance off the fairway was deemed lost. The jungle was just too dense and dangerous to have young women crawling through it looking for a wayward golf ball. So officials made it out of bounds and had marshals positioned at key points to signal back to the tee if a ball had gone out of play, forcing the players to take a penalty stroke and then play their third shot off the tee.

Emily describes the course as 'tight, horrible, unbelievably hard' and it broke nearly every player in the field, with tears a common sight, including from Lydia.

For Emily that tournament marked a low point in her amateur career as she struggled to hit the thin strips of grass between the jungle walls, and she admits she 'never really bounced back' from the beating the course gave her.

Lydia responded differently, making her teammates vow they would never again cry on the golf course out of frustration or let the pressure break them.

Emily was gobsmacked at how the youngster responded to the torture inflicted by the course.

'I think you only know someone's good when you get jealous of them. I'm only envious of the best and I looked at her and thought "God, you've got something everyone else wants" and realised then I was just playing for second.'

As if to prove she had been forged into a tougher competitor, Lydia went straight from the demands of India to beat Cecilia Cho in a two-hole sudden-death play-off to win the Australian Women's Strokeplay Championship in Melbourne, becoming the event's youngest winner. She rated the victory as among the best in her short but stunning amateur career, especially for the way she rebounded from the Queen Sirikit Cup. 'I wanted to do better here. I am quite proud of myself for what I have achieved.

'It's right up there with being top amateur at the professional tournaments,' she said, making a point of telling journalists it was her first win in a four-round tournament of the type she would play week in, week out as a professional.

Getting the victory over a great rival only added to the thrill, though a typically humble Lydia admitted the difficulty of taking victory at Cecilia's expense 'because we are such good friends'.

What's more, Lydia also battled a stomach bug she brought home from India and confessed to feeling awful during the final round. 'I've been throwing up this week and not feeling the best. Maybe the win will help me feel better.'

Coach Guy Wilson, acting as Lydia's caddy at the time, noted the extenuating circumstances around the win and he, too, took pride in the way his young charge rose above all the obstacles in her path and found a way to win.

'I guess we tend to forget that Lydia is thirteen,' recalled Wilson. 'But the way she handled herself and how she played in the play-off was a big step for her. She will learn now how to go about winning four-round tournaments.'

When the New Zealand Amateur Championship rolled around in April, at Russley Golf Club in Christchurch, Lydia went from strength to strength, scorching the field in the strokeplay section of the event. She beat Cecilia Cho by nine shots to take the top seeding into the match play, where she again made short work of her rivals to set up another national title showdown with her good friend, and second seed, who was looking for a hat-trick of titles.

This time it was Lydia who kept the mistakes at bay and when Cecilia made an error she pounced. On the 33rd hole of the scheduled 36-hole final, she claimed a 4&3 win (4 holes ahead with only 3 holes remaining) and Lydia's achievement write-ups gained another entry under the 'became the youngest . . .' list.

In beating Cecilia for the first time in a head-to-head match she became the youngest New Zealand Amateur champion. At 14 years and two days old she had nine months on Larissa Eruera when she won the title in 2008.

'It's one-all now,' Lydia said after the friendly rivals shared hugs and tears on the final green.

From there, Lydia, Cecilia and Emily Perry were joined by Chantelle Cassidy and Julianne Alvarez in the five-strong New Zealand team which spent most of June in Northern Ireland and Britain, contesting the British Amateur Championship and the Astor Cup, an international team event.

A blog put together by team manager Libby Steele for New Zealand Golf over the course of the trip featured regular first-person appearances from her young charges and Lydia's entries offer crucial insight into her character, her sense of humour and her ability to focus on positives, with words like 'fun' and 'enjoy' dotting her writing:

Sunday, June 5

Lydia: It was raining all day and we all got very dry . . . Not! All our gear turned saturated and we were cold and frozen as an ice block!!!! The course [Royal Portrush in County Antrim, Northern Ireland] is pretty but is very challenging with blowing, strong wind!!! Outside of the course just wanna say thank you Libby for shrinking our shirts . . . Don't blame the machine!!!! :) we went for a walk this morning and was about to take a photo with a cartoon turtle and Julianne put her hand in bird excrement! Very nice!!!! She tried to wipe it off in sand but didn't turn out any better :) The worst part of the day was having to play a six hour practice round in pouring rain while we were getting drenched!! Also thanks to the cows next door for waking us up in the morning . . . Thanks for the alarm call . . . Moooooooooooooooo.

Monday, June 6

Lydia: It didn't rain today!! Enjoyed playing today. I met my caddy, he is so cool. I think I can shoot many many under par! Yay! I didn't rip the course today, was too busy ripping my pants pocket!

Tuesday, June 7 — Round 1 qualifier

Libby: When I caught up with [Lydia] on the course, she gave me no golf updates as she was spinning in orbit having just met [Northern Ireland's US Open winner] Graeme McDowell!!

Lydia: I am off duty from all dishes because Graeme McDowell shook my hand . . . Hi Mum.

Wednesday, June 8 — Round 2 final qualifier

Libby: Lydia asks what's for dinner tomorrow — every night. I am unsure as to whether she likes the food or is hoping I will finally cook something she likes — and I'm too scared to ask. She also asked me to stop on the way home to get her a sim card. 10 minutes later she remembered that she did not even have a phone on this trip!!!

Lydia: Had fun in the rain today even tho the holes had ball repellent on them. I smiled all day so my mental game was a positive.

Thursday, June 9 — Round 1 British Amateur

Libby: Lydia played precision golf all morning and was always in complete control of her match. She attracted much ooohing and aaahing from the gallery. After 10 holes her comment to me was 'I have had only 2 pars and am 4 under. You do the math!!!!' She closed the match out on the 16th.

Friday, June 10

Lydia: Today was a different and exciting day! We went to Barry's amusement park, it was fun and interesting!

Saturday, June 11

Lydia: People in Ireland are so nice and all the buildings seem to have meaning to them.

Tuesday, June 14

Lydia: the course [Fairhaven in Liverpool] is very different to Royal Portrush. It has 365 bunkers — one for each day of the year!! I am confident about the next few days and want to bring home the Astor Cup for NZ.

Wednesday, June 15

Libby: Lydia had to do some putting practice before the afternoon round as she putted so little in the morning.

Lydia: I played solid today but unlucky for the singles match.

Thursday, June 16

Libby: Lydia came out in sizzling form to be 4 under the card at the turn and never let her opponent get a look in. Lydia 1-putted holes 5 through 9. Unbelievable distance control and putting display. She is gradually drawing in the galleries as the week progresses. Lydia commented that she knew she could do it after seeing her opponent play in the morning and knew her strengths and weaknesses.

Lydia: Enjoyed being partners with Julianne. Had a happy day!! We had Thai for dinner and are going back for more tomorrow!

Friday, June 17

Libby: Lydia said she felt angry at times during [her] match as after holing a 9m putt on 7 nothing would drop for her. She kept these emotions under control as I could not see them although her serious mode did go up a notch or 2 so my job was merely to make her laugh a little and try to keep her relaxed. She also said it was great to win all her matches today — quite an achievement when playing at number 1 against Australia!!

Lydia: I had a phenomenal day! Both my matches were challenging and exciting. It was good fun playing with a friendly rival!

At this stage, the eyes of the world hadn't fully focused on Lydia Ko. She'd made a name for herself in Australia and New Zealand, but creating any waves in the bigger pool of the United States was something else. Things would soon change when she tackled the US Amateur Championship in Rhode Island in August.

The US Amateur is where all wannabe golfers go to prove their worth as they step up the ladder of success. Lydia's Korean-Kiwi compatriot Danny Lee had made his name as the men's US Amateur champion in 2008 and there were high hopes Lydia would follow suit.

The US Amateur is decided in two stages: a four-round strokeplay tournament, which determines the top 64 seedings for the match play, followed by a knockout event which produces the champion.

Lydia didn't win the title — in fact she was knocked out in the second round — but she was equal top (co-medallist) in the strokeplay event, enough to catch the attention of *Golf Digest* for her first serious interview with a global golf outlet.

'I enjoy [golf],' she told *Golf Digest* after firing a five-under 66, the low round of the day at Rhode Island Country Club, 'but when I was six I'm pretty sure I enjoyed it more. It was less stressful.'

Lydia went on to tell *Golf Digest* she believed her young start in the game drove her performance. 'It's good to start at an early age. I think it's easier to learn when you're younger.'

The magazine concluded: 'While you may not have heard of Ko, she could be the next big thing in women's golf.'

A wrist injury Lydia brought home dampened the success, and she needed a minor operation to get rid of a ganglion, earning a well-needed two-month break from golf.

During her injury layoff, Lydia learned she had become — officially — the No. 1-ranked amateur in the world, leapfrogging Cecilia Cho. In the process she became the first female recipient of the Mark H McCormack Medal, a newly created annual award for the top-rated player in the women's world amateur rankings.

For Lydia, it was another box ticked on the long-term plan

laid down by her team, but that plan needed to change to keep pace with Lydia's evolving place in golf's landscape.

Guy Wilson felt that with Lydia having risen past Cecilia Cho and with no other rivals looming on the horizon, the New Zealand talent pool was now too small for his big fish. There was no one driving her to greater heights at home, so the plan was now to earn as many starts as possible in professional events. But for an amateur to get a place in a professional field required either the tournament sponsor or the host to issue an invitation, in much the same way as tennis tournaments offer wildcards to promising locals.

If Lydia was going to get into professional tournaments, the right people needed to know exactly who she was and what she could bring to their event.

Her status as the No. 1 amateur and coverage in *Golf Digest* was exactly what she needed. But she also needed to make a good impression on those in power, building contacts, cementing relationships and projecting herself into the minds of those who mattered.

'She just needs to get out there and represent herself,' said Guy Wilson of the press coverage that came with the US Amateur performance. 'The reality of this is it needs to be done for a player like this. You can't play anywhere else and get seen like this.'

He noted that people 'have met Lydia and seen she's the real deal. Although the trip has been expensive, these kinds of opportunities alone make it worthwhile. It's been really important for Lydia to be thrust into the limelight here.'

While thoughts of turning professional had slipped from under to on the radar, they were still a distant blip some years away from reality. The plan remained for Lydia to finish high school in Auckland and perhaps start university. She had her sights set on Stanford in California, where Tiger Woods and Michelle Wie had gone to university.

In remaining an amateur, Lydia couldn't recoup her expenses in prizemoney, so if she was going to travel the world looking for experience against professionals, she needed to find at least NZ$150,000 a year.

As she recovered from her injury, her team — in conjunction with New Zealand Golf — started work on raising funds to sit in a trust overseen by the sport's governing body.

It's common practice for New Zealand Golf to run trust funds on behalf of amateur players and they have dozens on the go at any time. But Lydia's trust fund was more actively promoted than many others thanks to her high public profile, along with Guy Wilson's ceaseless campaigning on the virtues of playing overseas and the high cost associated with preparing his charge for life as a professional.

Team Ko went into 2012 hoping to push the boundaries of Lydia's talent into uncharted territory — where they ended up was a place no amateur golfer had ever been before.

Chapter Seven

Bouncing back

There's an assumption Lydia won each time she teed off from an early age.

There's an element of truth to this but it's not the whole truth — in fact, if there's a pattern to her early amateur performances it's one step back, two steps forward.

It harks back to the first time she tried to hit her ball over the gully on the 15th hole at Titirangi as a seven-year-old . . . and failed. She tried again. And failed. Finally, she learned her lesson, adapted, came up with a plan and executed the correct play by chipping down towards the front of the gully to give herself a manageable distance across the chasm. It would have taken some humility — and common sense — not to mention maturity beyond her then seven years to realise doing the same thing over and over meant more balls in the gully.

The pattern repeated in the 2009 interprovincial event where she three-putted on the last green to cost her team victory, but she came out the following year, played undefeated, and led her crew to victory.

Her rivalry with Cecilia Cho was shaped by early defeats and it took some time for her to find a way past the older player, but once she did, she didn't look back.

In 2011 Lydia was the top seed at the Australian Women's Amateur Championship but lost in the second round; it was the same story in the 2011 US Amateur Championship — top seed but beaten in round two — and at the 2011 New South Wales Open she blew a one-shot lead on the final hole to lose to Caroline Hedwall.

In 2012, though, she was the bounce-back kid, turning all those lessons into a legacy as she skipped onto the world stage.

In January of that year, she became the first New Zealander since Jan Higgins in 1989 to win the Australian Women's Amateur Championship title, acknowledging afterwards the importance of making up for falling short the previous year. 'It feels pretty amazing and it feels great that I came further than I did last year so I'm pretty proud of myself.'

Totally self-aware, the 14-year-old recognised the momentous nature of her win and what it meant for her future: 'It is going to be nice to take this form into the professional events,' she said. 'People are going to start talking me up like I am going to win all the time . . . I don't know about that, but if I play like I played here this week, then I think I'm capable of coming in the top five in a pro event.'

The win earned Lydia entry to the prestigious Women's Australian Open at Royal Melbourne in February.

The Open, even though it's an Australian event, is part of

the America-based, global-focused Ladies Professional Golf Association. As Lydia's ultimate destination, to get a ticket on the fast train to the LPGA while still paying a kid's fare was crucial to what became a landmark year.

But before she ventured to the Australian Open, she had a return trip planned to the New South Wales Open at Oatlands, Sydney, in late January, where she hoped to atone for the previous year's loss.

Again she took the lead in the final round and again an older, seasoned professional came charging at her, this time playing partner Lindsey Wright, who vowed that as someone old enough to be Lydia's mother, 'I'm not letting this fourteen-year-old beat me.'

But Wright failed to realise that Lydia had been beating adults since she was seven, and as the pressure went on Lydia accelerated away, coming to the last hole with a four-shot lead.

With the pressure off, she came as close as she'd ever done to making a hole-in-one when her tee shot to the par-three closing hole hit the base of the flagstick.

Initially, reports had Lydia as the youngest woman to win a professional golf tournament, surpassing Amy Yang, who was 16 when she won the Australian Masters, by almost two years, but then people started digging and realised — scrub that — she had become the youngest winner of a professional golf tournament *ever*, male or female.

The previous record-holder, Japan's Ryo Ishikawa, was 15 when he won an event on the Japan Tour. Lydia was 14 years, nine months and five days old.

Asked for her reaction to the history-making win, Lydia could barely make sense of it: 'My mind's gone white — I can't really think much. All I know is I'm really happy. Making history is just amazing.

'I was nervous the whole round. I might not have showed it but I was sweating. I had to take some deep breaths and try and stay calm,' she said. 'It's phenomenal, I can't explain how I feel deep inside. To be part of history is like a miracle — it's not something you can have by clicking your fingers.'

Lydia has since been surpassed by Canadian Brooke Henderson, now also a rival on the LPGA Tour. At 14 years, nine months and three days, Henderson was just two days younger than Lydia when she won a 36-hole event on the Canadian Tour, which is not regarded as quite being in the same league as winning a standard professional event played over 54 or 72 holes.

Guy Wilson, for a man who had made it his life's mission to guide a young girl to a professional triumph, reacted in somewhat muted fashion to his charge's success, perhaps setting the scene for the way the Ko camp would downplay many of her ensuing successes as the first steps on a long journey.

'At this stage a win is a win, most of them don't really rank much higher than each other,' Wilson said. 'It's not for money, it's not for any reward, for her it's just a matter of getting out there and playing golf.'

Next stop was the Australian Women's Masters, where Lydia would come face to face with another prodigy, American starlet Lexi Thompson. Thompson had incredibly qualified for the US Open as a 12-year-old, turned pro at 15 and had set a record of her own as the youngest winner on the LPGA Tour (Amy Yang's win was not on the LPGA Tour) at 16 years, seven months and eight days.

Unlike the diminutive Ko, Lexi is an obvious athlete, standing 1.83 metres and hammering the ball as far as some male professionals.

The two teenagers met on the practice range at Royal Pines,

home of the Australian Ladies Masters, on the Gold Coast on a Tuesday afternoon as photographers clamoured for pics of the Amazonian Lexi Thompson and the bespectacled Asian girl destined to one day erase Lexi's name from the record books.

Young Lydia benefited from having targets to chase in New Zealand — from Sharon Ahn to Cecilia Cho — and Lexi played the same role: a gazelle in the eyes of the tiger, with Guy Wilson revealing Lexi and her manager Bobby Kreusler had both been an inspiration and motivation for the Ko team. Wilson had met with Kreusler the previous year at the Australian Open and acknowledged that Lexi's experience in the United States had guided his selection of the events Lydia should play in.

Lydia finished the Australian Masters as leading amateur and in a tie for 32nd place after a disappointing final round of two-over 74 . . . but there may have been a reason she wasn't quite so focused. Before she teed off she received an email advising she had been invited to compete in both the US Amateur Championship and the US Open. The invitations came because organisers wanted her in their events and didn't wish to risk the fact she might not qualify. They were fast-tracking her into the field because of her appeal. It meant her team didn't have to spend extra money trying to qualify for either event. It meant their plan to get noticed was working just fine.

At the next stop, the Australian Open on the famed Royal Melbourne course, Guy Wilson revealed another small gem about his star pupil and the way they were working. 'We've been concentrating on her using her imagination a lot more,' he said at the time. 'Gold Coast [the venue for the Australian Ladies Masters] was very one-dimensional. It didn't require much thinking, it was see a yardage and hit it. Here there are three or four options around the green.'

That type of imaginative play suited Lydia a lot more; it was the style of golf she'd been taught from a young age by her dad and which John Lister embossed. Playing on tricky courses that required adaptation and clever management was her forte, and she proved as much by out-thinking many leading professionals to finish the Open tied for 19th (again as leading amateur). She was ahead of such global talents as Lexi Thompson, Suzann Pettersen, Karrie Webb, Mo Martin, Angela Stanford and Morgan Pressel. In a world-class field full of major champions past and future, the 14-year-old Kiwi was right at home.

Gregg Thorpe, New Zealand Golf's talent and coach development manager, said Lydia's quick adaptation to the upper reaches of women's golf came as no surprise to those who had been grooming her for just this stage.

'For some players it can take a year or two to adapt to the elevated level of professional competition, but it's never really fazed Lydia. She now has two years of experience at this level, and this experience along with her superbly consistent golf game is helping her to forge a path like no other.'

John Lister never doubted Lydia's destination would be the top, but what surprised him was how quickly his Sunday morning protégée had accelerated.

'I've always thought New Zealand provided a good grounding for golfers,' Lister says; 'because of our size, it's possible to climb the ladder here — so when you go out into the world, you know how to work your way up . . . but when Lydia left New Zealand, she just went straight to the top rung of the ladder.'

By now the murmurings about this talented teen had reached the ears of major media organisations and when Lydia returned home from Australia to compete in the New Zealand Open, television news networks, a current affairs programme, radio stations and newspaper journalists swamped her — no small feat in a rugby-obsessed country.

Lydia, fast revealing herself as an old soul in a teenager's body, said the swarm of media was just another facet of the game she had to learn to deal with rather than resent. What was once an onerous task for a young girl whose English was not quite perfect now became a chance to charm and influence the hard-bitten cynics who make up the ranks of New Zealand sports journalism.

She was at ease with scribes who found her thoughtful, funny and intelligent. At 14, she was not a giggly, shy girl but a confident, outgoing teenager who understood her success and the obligations that came with it.

And with an openness and self-awareness beyond her years, she offered a rare insight into the demands golf placed on her life, wistfully assessing what she'd had to give up as a teenager pursuing golf at the highest level.

'Golf is like 99.9 per cent of my life, and then there's school,' she said. 'I don't get much time to go out with my friends. I always wanted to go to my best friend's party, I always wanted to have a sleepover, or go to the movies with my friends, but there haven't been many times when I've been able to do that. They're the sacrifices I have made.'

The interview session also allowed her and Guy Wilson to open a window on their coach/caddy–player relationship, as they engaged in friendly banter much like brother and sister. Asked if Wilson was her caddy or her coach during the weeks he carried her bag, Lydia mulled it over before yelling out to Wilson, who was doing his own interview, 'Are you my coach or my caddy on the course?' Wilson replied: 'You're my boss, aren't you?'

'Yeah, so he's my caddy. Yeah, I'm the boss on the course.'

It was something Wilson would learn only too well in the near future.

At 14, she was not a giggly, shy girl but a confident, outgoing teenager who understood her success and the obligations that came with it.

Maybe all the pressure of the media attention that week of the New Zealand Open took something out of Lydia, but for once in her recent run of professional events she didn't finish leading amateur, falling one shot behind her old sparring partner Cecilia Cho, now 17. Australian Lindsey Wright took the title.

Following the Open, Cecilia bade farewell to the amateur ranks — and to New Zealand — turning professional after the tournament and returning to Korea.

While acknowledging how much she would miss New Zealand, Cecilia allowed herself a moment of honest reflection, noting it would be nice to go back to Korea to become just one among hundreds of talented professionals and to get out of the 'spotlight' for a while.

Lydia acknowledged how the rivalry had improved her as she said goodbye to her friend.

'Her playing good improved my game and hopefully me playing good improved her game. She is soon going and it is quite sad. She has been a friendly rival and I am going to miss her.'

With Cecilia out of the picture, competition for Lydia fell away dramatically, as she proved in winning the Muriwai Open in Auckland by an almost incomprehensible 17 shots over New Zealand teammate Emily Perry. 'I have no idea how much I won by,' she said, proving how contained she'd become in her own world.

She also noted how much she enjoyed playing at the wind-blasted Muriwai links set-up. 'I seem to play the best here on the windiest days — I must be a wind-girl or something.'

That tournament also featured an important milestone in Lydia's evolution, with a decision made during that week that she should stop using Guy Wilson as her caddy so he could focus solely on coaching.

The move came amid fears Wilson was trying to wear too many hats, with Lydia's old Sunday morning playing partner John Lister among the critics.

'Guy was trying to be everything — coach, manager, caddy,' says Lister, who was asked to break the news to Wilson by Lydia's mum Tina. 'I told him he shouldn't be caddying any more. "What's she going to do without me?" he said. I told him she probably knew more than him anyway and at some stage you have to let them do it themselves.

'He was like an overprotective father. I spent an hour with him and said what I'm trying to do is protect your job as coach — one day Lydia is going to tell you to get out of her life; just stick to your job as a coach.'

The official line was that the arrangement was designed to give Lydia a fresh approach and the chance to make her own decisions without relying on Wilson so much.

With his caddying duties behind him, Wilson kept working on Lydia's technique, instilling some minor swing changes to ensure the wrist problem she suffered in 2011 didn't recur.

That meant changing the way Lydia gripped the club, a fundamental part of the way any golfer sets up for a shot. It was a major change and it's a testament to Lydia's ability that she was able to incorporate such an overhaul of her basic technique without losing any momentum.

Guy Wilson also had to alter Lydia's swing to account for how much she'd grown in her teen years. As she grew taller and stronger, the technical specifications of the clubs changed: their length, the flex of the shaft, the loft (angle of the club face), the grip thickness, the weight. It couldn't have been easy to maintain top form while going through this metamorphosis, yet Lydia barely batted an eyelid, taking her rewired swing into her major championship debut at the US Women's Open at Kohler,

Wisconsin, and finishing — predictably — as top amateur and tied for 39th.

The tournament, her first at this level, brought its share of pressure: 'I was lining up my putt on the first hole and my hands were shaking. I just couldn't putt my line straight.' But again it was about learning — about playing different kinds of shots and managing and coping with stress. Unlike many professionals, however, Lydia could quell her nerves without worrying about losing any money, something that had to work to her advantage in the future.

Continuing the theme of 2012 being her bounce-back year, Lydia went on from the US Open to seeking to win the US Amateur Championship in August, at the Country Club course in Cleveland, Ohio.

After working her way through the 64-strong field in the knockout stage, Lydia came up against American Jaye Marie Green in the 36-hole final, where Lydia showed uncanny faith in her ability on a critical hole.

Having led one-up after the first 18 holes, Lydia found herself under attack as Jaye Marie played aggressively, but she answered every question the American asked and held her lead, increasing it each time her opponent made any small error.

On the 27th hole, a par three, Lydia had one of the hardest bunker shots in golf, from a downhill lie on damp sand with a steep face in front of her and only a small portion of green on which to land her ball.

As Lydia surveyed her shot, her ever-present mother was heard to say: 'Try that flop bunker shot that you practise for fun. Be aggressive. Pretend it's a practice shot.'

Lydia obeyed the instruction and hit a perfect shot, the ball riding a spray of sand to land right by the hole. This left her a simple par putt to maintain a four-up margin, which proved critical as Jaye Marie kept attacking on the final nine holes.

Lydia held firm and eventually closed out the match 3&1, drawing widespread admiration, not least from her opponent Jaye Marie, who couldn't help but enjoy the moment despite the loss. 'Lydia has such a great attitude in that she laughs at everything and she's fun to play with.'

It says something about Lydia that she could maintain that outwardly positive and light-hearted approach while burning with desire inwardly, noting afterwards that she 'wanted to win that so badly'. And in doing so, she shed a few tears. 'It's the first time I have been emotional at golf. I think that was due to my complete focus, and a bit of exhaustion.'

Like so many of her other triumphs this one also came with a special incentive that inspired her — with Tina promising Lydia she could meet her favourite Korean movie star, Ji Sub So, if she could become the first New Zealand woman to win the prestigious US title. It's typical of the way Tina has inspired her daughter over the years, from the offer of $100 if an eight-year-old Lydia could make an eagle, to allowing her to get her ears pierced after finishing top amateur at the New Zealand Open for the first time.

Quite how Tina engineered a meeting with such a famous actor is something of a mystery, but in another two weeks it might have been a case of Ji Sub So asking to meet Lydia Ko.

Chapter Eight
O Canada

The Canadian Open is one of the most prestigious tournaments in women's golf. From 1979 to 2001 it held its place as one of the LPGA's four major championships. It lost its status when the women's game became truly global in the twenty-first century, replaced by the Women's British Open, but remains one of the richest women's tournaments in the world. As a result, it always draws a top-quality field.

In August 2012 it became a proving ground in the fast-paced evolution of Lydia Ko, another chance to play in a professional tournament, another opportunity to learn the ropes inside the roped-off fairways of the money-driven LPGA.

But the stepping-stone plan envisaged by her team suddenly looked like a well-paved bridge as the 15-year-old surged to the front of the pack after the third round. Typically, as the media queued up to question the Kiwi kid at the Vancouver Golf Club on the eve of the final round, Lydia shrugged off her achievement and reasserted her fun mantra.

'To be up there is just an honour, especially playing against the world's best. Fifteen-year-olds don't lead at an LPGA event all the time. I'm very surprised.

'Today I tried to have more fun, but my score wasn't as good. I mean, seventy-two is better than seventy-three or any other score, so I'm pretty happy.'

Lydia admitted it was nerve-wracking, but said, 'I'm really here for experience and fun, and I'm having fun at the moment. If I don't win tomorrow, I don't think I'll be disappointed. If I do win, I'll take it like an honour.

'I can't concentrate on what the other players are doing. If they shoot sixty-six and I shoot sixty-eight and I lose, I can't control what they do. So I'm just going to play my game and have one shot at a time.

'You can't play perfect golf,' she added, as she headed for the practice green to prepare for a final round showdown with the world No. 2, American Stacy Lewis, and soon-to-be world No. 1 Inbee Park from Korea.

Lydia didn't play perfect golf in the final round, but she turned in an almost flawless performance as she distanced some of the world's best players to win by three shots. In doing so, she provoked responses which ranged from shock to awe, not to mention a few furrowed brows of disappointment from the handful of Canadians who knew Lydia's family had originally been toying with moving to their country. As they celebrated her triumph, they also rued the big catch that got away.

Without coach Guy Wilson there as her caddy, Lydia picked up a local club member, Brian Alexander, as her course guide and bag carrier. 'I didn't have to do anything,' Alexander said. 'I just stood back in awe. It was a remarkable performance.'

For her win Lydia earned nothing. She left behind a winner's cheque of US$300,000, which went to a grateful Inbee Park. As leading amateur, Lydia's non-cash prize was a coffee-maker — symbolic of a golfing world waking up and smelling the coffee — but in terms of buying publicity for herself, the win was worth far more than the prizemoney she had to forgo.

Rival and playing partner Stacy Lewis couldn't believe her eyes, commenting, 'I was most impressed with her demeanour. You would have never known it was the final round of an LPGA event. She played like she had been there before. It was an impressive round for an LPGA pro, let alone a fifteen-year-old.'

As Lydia homed in on victory, she said Stacy provided great support, chatting to the teen as they walked up the 18th fairway, the only time all day Lydia showed any nerves as her adrenaline got the best of her and she overshot the green with her approach shot and ended up making a bogey.

If her amazing play hadn't won over each and every fan in sight, Lydia's trophy acceptance afterwards certainly did. Fresh, amusing, at ease, saying all the right things . . . she was adorable. And as she finished the crowd let out a giant 'awwwww'.

With the Canadian Open win, which made her the youngest titleholder in the history of the LPGA, Lydia was propelled firmly into the international spotlight, with the obvious question being — given she'd had to sacrifice US$300,000 — whether she would turn professional sooner than planned.

But Lydia was adamant she would stay on the road mapped out by her family and team, even if that meant she was going at a slightly slower speed than her powerful golfing engine was capable of achieving.

'This is a great win, but I don't think this will affect me,

Youngest golfers to win an LPGA event

- Lydia Ko, 2012 Canadian Women's Open (72-hole event) at 15 years, 4 months, 2 days.
- Lexi Thompson, 2011 Navistar LPGA Classic (72-hole event) at 16 years, 8 months, 8 days.
- Marlene Hagge, 1952 Sarasota Open (18-hole event) at 18 years, 14 days.
- Marlene Hagge, 1952 Bakersfield Open (18-hole event) at 18 years, 2 months, 15 days.
- Paula Creamer, 2005 Sybase Classic (72-hole event) at 18 years, 9 months, 17 days.
- Morgan Pressel, 2007 Kraft Nabisco Championship (72-hole event) at 18 years, 10 months, 9 days.
- Paula Creamer, 2005 Evian Masters (72-hole event) at 18 years, 11 months, 18 days.
- Amy Alcott, 1975 Orange Blossom Classic (54-hole event) at 19 years, 1 day.

changing my routes to my career. My mum and dad will probably be the ones to choose the time when I do turn pro. Obviously, actually collecting that [money] would have been nice. I wouldn't mind having the cheque but that's life and you can't get everything you want.'

For a young woman who had spent her life going without things she wanted in order to focus on golf, it was par for the course, it seemed, to pleasantly forgo what would be a life-changing sum of money for any other 15-year-old.

'She just shrugs it off, not realising exactly what she's done,' said her coach Guy Wilson, who wasn't in Canada but caught up with Lydia via Skype.

Wilson also opened another small window into the way Lydia Ko ticks by revealing a trick he used to encourage her to feel more positive about her sometimes unreliable putting.

Ahead of the tournament, Lydia had been a little 'negative' about her putting so Wilson told her go online and Google herself until she found 20 quotes from articles praising her short game.

Following her Canadian Open win, it would have taken about a nanosecond to find another 20 positive Lydia Ko references, as the world gushed with praise for the teenager.

Dottie Pepper, one of the greats of the women's game who has the ear of America's golf fans as a commentator on the men's PGA tour, said after the win: 'This kid is an absolute rock star. [Kiwi caddy] Steve Williams told me two years ago to watch out for this kid. Come on, now. She's barely 13 years old. You want me to watch out for who? And sure enough, her name started rising as her stock rose. It's been pretty amazing to watch.'

Judy Rankin, who won the Missouri State Amateur at 14, called the event as an analyst for Golf Channel. Asked whether

Lydia could win the Women's British Open at Royal Liverpool a few weeks later, Rankin replied: 'It wouldn't be the biggest shock. This was no fluke.'

With all the success of 2012, there also came an intense focus not just on what Lydia had done but on what she'd sacrificed.

She literally had no childhood as most people would understand it. Outside of school, when she wasn't travelling, she was totally immersed in golf. She trained morning, noon and night. There was little or no time for movies, trips away or sleepovers.

A typical day at home in Auckland would start at 5.30 am, with fitness work in the morning before she'd head to school. At lunchtime her mum would pick her up and take her to the driving range for a short practice before returning her to school.

After school she was straight back to the driving range — this time for a session with Guy Wilson to work on an element of her game before heading to the North Shore Golf Club to practise on the course. She described the work she did in the late afternoon as 'intense . . . it's how I've become a good player'.

When darkness fell there would be a third trip back to the driving range for a session under lights, with Lydia — like Se Ri Pak in Korea 20 years earlier — not leaving until she was happy with whatever technical aspect she was working on.

Usually she'd be home by 8 pm, but sometimes it was much later. Dinner was followed by homework, which sometimes pushed her past midnight.

Away from school, when she was on the road in the US or Europe, again there was no chance of actually travelling in the way others understand it. Wherever she went in the world — from Ireland, to Turkey, to India, to America — she never got to see the sights or enjoy the cities she was in. Entire days were spent at the golf course, practising or playing, and in the reverse of what happened at home in Auckland, schooling was slotted into gaps in the golf agenda. She would keep up with her classes via a log-in to the school's remote learning system.

The way the Ko family structured the business of her golf meant that while she didn't get much time with friends or doing other leisure activities, neither did she have to do the usual chores other teenagers would be expected to carry out.

'Washing dishes, cleaning and cooking are not my responsibilities,' she said. 'I could do these things, but if you were me, would you take away six hours of golf practice each week in exchange for doing chores? As a family, we've decided the answer to that is a firm "no".'

Six hours a week doing chores would have represented close to 10 per cent of the time she dedicated to golf, with Guy Wilson estimating she put in 50 hours a week. In sport, where athletes talk of the 'one percenters' that can make a difference between winning and losing, that kind of commitment makes a huge difference.

Maintaining such an unrelenting dedication to the game was a trade-off, Lydia figured. She loved the game of golf and thrived in a competitive environment, but like anyone who commits a large chunk of her life to a single-minded pursuit there were times when she pined for another life. Yet she was mature enough to understand she couldn't have it both ways — either she was going to be one of the best golfers in the world, or she was going to have a normal life.

'My life seems to be golf, golf, golf, golf, golf,' she said in a sing-song voice on New Zealand current affairs show *Close-Up* in 2012. 'I miss seeing my friends, going to movies . . . Last year I was like oh God, I want to see my friends but my parents keep

‘I guess the main losses to my life are not being able to go out with friends, not being able to socialise and function like most girls my age. Instead, I’ve had to grow up quickly on the golf course.’

telling me if you make a sacrifice then something you want to achieve will come.

'I guess the main losses to my life are not being able to go out with friends, not being able to socialise and function like most girls my age. Instead, I've had to grow up quickly on the golf course.'

At 15, when others might be earning pocket money at McDonald's, golf was her fulltime job — it's just that she didn't get paid for it.

The pressure, the lack of a normal childhood, caused raised eyebrows over how hard the teen was being pushed — or pushing herself.

Even Guy Wilson acknowledged Lydia's life was anything but normal for someone of her age. 'She doesn't spend time with her friends, she doesn't go to the mall, she doesn't celebrate Christmas holidays. Is she a normal kid? No, not by any means,' he said on the back of her win in the Canadian Open. 'Since Lydia was six, golf is all she has known.'

What kept Lydia on track in these demanding years was the unwavering commitment of her parents.

When she was at home, Gil Hong oversaw her independent training and when she travelled Tina was there every step of the way. She was a mother, manager, chauffeur, cook, counsellor, washerwoman, roommate, bag-carrier and confidante.

Tina, as witnessed during the US Amateur, would also give on-course advice, as well as offer incentives to keep her daughter on track. Pocket money was determined by how well she played, with Tina doling out $10 for every shot under par Lydia achieved in a tournament — so a 10-under-par performance would earn her $100.

'My parents, they've done so many great things for me. I'm always thankful even though sometimes I don't really say it.'

Another release valve for Lydia was the fact she really did have fun in the golf environment. Counting the number of times Lydia has used the word 'fun' in her press conferences is a bit like counting stars in the night sky — it was her mantra.

It was more than a mind trick, as she genuinely loved the golfing environment.

Ryan Fox, who was the number one male amateur when Lydia ruled the female ranks in New Zealand, spent a lot of time alongside Lydia and can vouch for her approach.

'From a very young age her passion for the game hasn't changed at all — with a lot of people it does. From doing it for fun to doing it for a job, her passion hasn't changed.'

Again, Lydia's parents had a vital role to play in keeping a firm hand on Lydia's back to ensure she was moving forward, but never creating so much pressure it became intolerable.

'From what I saw there was no external pressure,' Fox says, 'and if you had a whole bunch of external pressure you couldn't be in that mindset. You can't enjoy it when you're under pressure.'

In searching for the secrets to Lydia's success, there's one place you cannot overlook: the Institute of Golf — iGolf — on Auckland's North Shore.

Founded by golf teacher Craig Dixon, physiotherapist Brad Takai and mental skills coach David Niethe in 2008, it offers a wrap-around service for golfers, and Lydia was fast becoming the best advertisement for the place.

An entire team of people were working with Lydia, and other promising players such as Michael Hendry, rather than the golfer having to find a series of service providers, some of whom might be at odds with each other — or at least not on the same page.

The institute was the first of its kind in New Zealand and it meant Lydia had a swing coach in Guy Wilson, who could rely on her mental trainer David Niethe not to inadvertently undermine or confuse the messages. And the physical trainer and the physiotherapist also knew what Wilson was trying to achieve so they developed their plans around Lydia's physical wellbeing to match the grand scheme.

Dixon said the establishment of the Institute of Golf came at a perfect time for Lydia, who at 12 was the ideal age to benefit from mental and physical conditioning. After Lydia's Canadian Open win, he said 'We're stoked; we feel like we've helped her as a team.'

It also took Lydia outside the framework of New Zealand Golf and with it helped change New Zealand Golf's approach to coaching.

Previously, and by default, talented amateurs would have fallen under New Zealand Golf's umbrella when it came to coaching, but Guy Wilson wanted to keep Lydia away from another set-up, saying any input from New Zealand Golf would confuse things for her and would have added an unnecessary layer to what the Institute of Golf was already doing quite well.

Almost because of Lydia, and other talented amateurs such as Cecilia Cho, New Zealand Golf, rather than trying to re-coach these players, instead opted to support the primary coaching team. In effect, the governing body stepped away from what New Zealand Golf's Gregg Thorpe called 'technical intervention' to instead offer inspiration and assistance.

'In terms of the impact we've had on Lydia? We're secondary service providers, a part of her service provision team,' Thorpe said. 'We'd love to share the kudos for the development of Lydia equally with iGolf. The time and energy Guy has put in and the other guys at iGolf, without that it wouldn't have happened.

But we are certainly a part of that and our programmes are an important part of that relationship.'

In other words, Lydia Ko almost singlehandedly changed the way the national golf body organised its coaching.

The holistic approach developed at the Institute of Golf meant that anything Lydia did was informed by the other people in the team around her. When she practised, she didn't hit ball after ball in a mindless fashion; just the opposite, she brought a mindfulness to her routine.

She never hit a golf ball for the sake of it; she hit it with a purpose, to either practise a particular shot or to work on a technical aspect of her swing. And when she wasn't practising a shot or going through a routine, she switched off and relaxed, shared jokes with those around her, chatted with friends or fellow competitors, and listened to music. When it came time to step back into practice mode, she shut out the distractions and brought her incredible focus to the task at hand.

Along with her clubs, that skill of mental compartmentalisation came with her onto the golf course, as so many of her rivals have come to learn. Intense concentration on shots would give way to chit-chat as she walked the fairway.

'It's hard to explain how she does it,' says Ryan Fox. 'She was good fun to play a round of golf with — she'd engage you between shots and chat away, but then snap back into the zone and hit her golf shot with purpose.'

That ability to be a fierce competitor one minute and laughing, chatting teen the next was captured in a feature profile for the *New York Times* which appeared during the British Open in July 2012, when Lydia tied for 17th — yet another remarkable feat given it was only the second time she'd teed it up in a major championship. Again, she finished leading amateur.

'Appearances can be deceiving with Ko, who is 5 feet 6 inches, with a round face framed by black-rimmed glasses. Her unguarded smile, compulsive giggling and tendency to view life as one big loving cup overflowing with awesomeness cast her as your typical teenager . . .' The feature gave an amusing description of Lydia's behaviour when walking with her mother from the media centre to the clubhouse. 'Ko draped herself over her mother's back like a sweater, crossed her arms around her mother's neck and held on tightly. When Tina Ko bent at the waist, Lydia's feet left the ground and her laughter drowned out the wind.'

After her outstanding performance at the British Open in July and her Canadian Open win in August, Lydia came down to earth with a relative thud when she was reunited with New Zealand teammates Emily Perry and Munchin Keh in September 2012 at the Espirito Santo tournament in Antalya, Turkey.

Manager Libby Steele again wrote a blog for the New Zealand Golf website and Lydia's entries reveal yet another side of this burgeoning superstar. While she talks a little about her own game, her comments are almost entirely focused on her teammates, the team itself, and peripheral humour such as New Zealand Golf high performance manager Gregg Thorpe ordering cheesecake only to be delivered a cheese salad. ('His dreams of a scrumptious cheesecake were over. Now he has a plate of untouched cheese salad! Now we all know what we will get when we order a cheesecake! Mmmmm I miss NZ cheesecake!')

But not once did Lydia talk about herself, how well she was playing. The New Zealand team tied with Spain for fifth place, but Lydia walked away from Turkey with yet another title to her name as the leading individual, effectively the world amateur champion.

In a sporting world where superstars wear their massive egos like a crown, Lydia is just the opposite — and it's not feigned humility either.

'She's not a talker,' says Ryan Fox. 'She doesn't make bold statements that she's going to do this or that, she's just Lydia and goes about her business. What she does talk about is having fun and she does.'

The magnitude of what Lydia achieved in 2012, a four-of-a-kind crown of amateur titles in New Zealand, Australia, the United States and then the world individual title at Espirito Santo, as well as wins in two professional tournaments as an amateur, is about as good as it gets in golf. As an amateur she'd scaled the highest peaks available to her — and her sights were now on Everest.

Yet the niggling question remained as to whether she needed more time at base camp.

On examining whether she should turn pro sooner rather than later, Guy Wilson pointed out the LPGA Tour had an entry age limit of 18 and so even if Lydia turned professional ahead of schedule, she would have to rely on what are known as sponsor's exemptions — where the tournament backers can include a small number of players of their choice — in order to play.

He also worried whether Lydia was worldly-wise enough to be let loose in the cut-throat professional world. 'I think Lydia needs to do a bit of living first, which is why she still wants to go to a US college — she sees it as a chance to be self-sufficient. She has led a bit of a sheltered life. I noticed when we road-tripped in the States that she was oblivious to stuff like how much things cost.'

Chapter Nine

Avoiding burnout

Before Lydia Ko there was Michelle Wie.

Tall, attractive, athletic, powerful — good enough as a teenager to play well against men and acquit herself with pride.

Like Lydia, the American is generation 1.5, born in Hawaii to immigrant Korean parents, with her father a professor at the University of Hawaii and her mother a top golfer.

At the age of 11, Michelle almost qualified to make the main field at the PGA Tour's Sony Open — you read that right: she almost played in a PGA Tour event against men when she was just 11.

When she turned pro at 16, she was an immediate drawcard but she also drew negativity to her like a magnet. She failed to sign scorecards, didn't know all the rules of golf, said outrageous things, received exemptions to enter events on both the PGA and LPGA tours — and when she didn't actually live up to the hype she earned the moniker 'Little Miss Too Much Too Soon' and drew comparisons to tennis player Anna Kournikova as having more style than substance.

Michelle was famous before she got results and then derided for not getting the results her hype suggested she should. Her parents were accused of hothousing her. Compared with Lydia's entry into the world of golf — under the radar and then letting her clubs do the talking — the Michelle Wie Show was all fanfare and confetti.

And then, bit by bit, Wie broke down.

Her list of illnesses is as along as Lydia's list of wins — infections, bad ankles, bursitis in her hip and, most controversially, a wrist injury at 18 that forced her out of golf for four months but which some players have claimed she contrived to escape the world of golf for a while.

Wie grew to hate golf. The game had robbed her of her youth. She lived a cossetted life, protected by her parents and the confines of the golf world. After the wrist injury she tried to find a normal balance and spent almost five years mixing golf and education by attending Stanford University. The studies restricted how much she practised and played, but she managed both worlds with aplomb.

While the injuries still linger — much the product of her extreme swing mechanics — she came back to golf rejuvenated (albeit with the weirdest putting stance on the planet) and finally won a major, the 2013 US Open.

What's the difference between Wie and Ko? Why at 18 was Michelle Wie washed up and looking to break out of golf and find another life, while Lydia seemed to sail on unharmed and unhurt?

The difference is all to do with burnout. Michelle Wie had burned out at 18. Despite a punishing schedule that has seen her playing at the top level since she was just 14, Lydia has escaped it.

Renowned coach David Leadbetter, who would soon have a closer understanding of Lydia Ko, had been Michelle Wie's coach when things went wrong and he sounded a word of warning about the amount of golf Lydia was playing at 15 and 16 years of age. 'This girl's impressive,' Leadbetter said. 'You just hope they don't push the burnout button.'

Pam Greenhalgh, who got to know Lydia when she first stepped up to play for the North Harbour interprovincial team at the age of 10, also worried she was going too high too soon.

'I always worried about burnout . . . that she'd lose her childhood,' Greenhalgh says. 'We've all heard the stories of Tiger Woods and [tennis star] Andre Agassi and I don't think I'd wish that on my children because you don't get those years back; if you invest that much time, and the parents invest that much time and all turns to pot . . .'

Teammate Emily Perry also had concerns Lydia took on more than she could handle. 'When we were younger and just starting off I was worried she might burn out because none of us could keep up with her, but she obviously had something slightly different going on. She didn't have any distractions — she was free just to go for it and put all her eggs into one basket.'

The secret to avoiding burnout, it seems, is simple — focus on playing for fun rather than winning.

Professor Ken Hodge, an expert in sport psychology at Otago University's School of Physical Education, Sport and Exercise Sciences, describes golf as an 'absolutely brutal sport from a mental perspective'. Think of how many promising players fall by the wayside and you would have to agree. Yet, for Lydia, despite the demands on her, there genuinely seemed to be nothing else she would rather have done as a teenager; movies and sleepovers be damned.

'I've used her [example] a lot to highlight different types of motivations and how successful some people can be when they're not obsessed with winning — and how enjoyment is not a soft option,' Hodge says.

'I use a quote from her when she said something like: "I can't think about the money — I can only control my score, I can't control my opponents, I play better when I'm smiling and enjoying myself." For someone that young to arrive at that understanding and self-awareness, to know what helps her play well and to not be bullied or coerced into thinking otherwise by the media, fans or sponsors is quite amazing. She's a remarkable young woman.'

Factors that can lead to burnout are loss of motivation and the search for perfection, while factors counting against burnout are what's known as athlete engagement, optimism and passion. Over-training also has a bearing on burnout.

The key drivers of motivation are what psychologists call autonomy and competence.

Autonomy is an athlete having a sense of volition and choice in what they do, that they are in charge of their own fate and in control of where they are going. If Lydia didn't feel in control — if she felt forced to play — her motivation would drop and burnout would come into play.

Competence is just that — to be good at something — but golf has an unusual measure of competence because it's essentially a game you play against yourself. There's no direct opponent, as in tennis or rugby, who is trying to thwart you or make you react. You are completely in charge of your destiny and the score you shoot is governed by how well you perform certain processes, especially under pressure. Therefore, because you can't control your opponent, or what they shoot, in many ways you can't control the outcome of the competition. So when it comes to competence in golf, counter-intuitively, the key is not to be results-focused.

'If your only measure of competence is whether you are beating someone, then you don't have any control over that because in golf you can't control how the other person is performing,' Hodge says.

Worrying about aspects you cannot control, such as an opponent you can't influence directly, can become a source of stress and worry for a player. The key for Lydia is to play against herself and that's reflected in the way she regularly states what she thinks she should shoot in a round of golf. For instance, when she successfully defended her Canadian Open title in 2013, she told reporters: 'My goal today was to shoot five-under and just play my own game. If somebody else shot better, then I can't do anything about it.'

By focusing on shooting a score that is in her control, depending on how she's hitting the ball and how the weather or the course is presenting itself, Lydia doesn't get bound up in the actual business of winning. Winning is a by-product of what she's trying to do — match a target she's created for herself. It's a stress-free, self-contained way to play a round of golf. And Lydia has learned that she plays best when she's relaxed and having fun so she constantly taps into that.

'That's one of the keys as to why she's so level headed,' suggests Ken Hodge. 'She focuses on the things she can control, shooting a score, enjoying herself out there. Everyone wants to win, that's a given; the key focus should be on how to win. The process that leads to winning, if you like.'

Hodge likened the mindset to the one employed by swimmer

While she will do everything she can to create the best possible shot, or outcome, she accepts perfectionism is impossible in the notoriously fickle world of golf.

golf
golf

previous page

Lydia Ko burst into public awareness as a 12-year-old when she was runner-up in the final of the New Zealand Amateur Championship to rival Cecilia Cho. FAIRFAX MEDIA NZ

above

Lydia with her dad, Gil Hong Ko, a huge influence in her career, especially with his approach to practice which focused on fun, variety and continuous challenges for his daughter. FAIRFAX MEDIA NZ

above

Lydia's mum Tina has been a constant companion throughout her career — chauffeur, chef, cleaner and confidante. NEW ZEALAND HERALD/NEWSPIX.CO.NZ

following spread

Lydia lines up a putt at the NZ Open at Pegasus in 2012 under the watchful eye of Guy Wilson, her coach until 2013. PHOTOSPORT

Titleist
KO
ISPS HANDA

top

Lydia is often seen laughing on the golf course — even when she makes a mistake. She says laughing is better than getting angry at herself. GETTY IMAGES

bottom

Lydia uses a technique called Aim Point to line up her putts — it involves using her feet to feel how much slope a green has and then translating that into using one, two or three fingers to measure how much her putt will break, and therefore where to aim. GETTY IMAGES

top

Lydia shot a final round of nine-under-par 63 to become the youngest woman winner of a major title at the Evian Championship in France in 2015. GETTY IMAGES

bottom

It has become a tradition that the winner of the year's first major, the ANA Inspiration, plunges into Poppie's Pond beside the 18th green at Mission Hills Country Club in California. Lydia is pictured in the water in March 2016 with her caddy Jason Hamilton, her sister Sura and mum Tina. GETTY IMAGES

following page

Lydia draped herself in the New Zealand flag after winning the 2015 Evian Championship, her first major. She calls herself a Kowi — Korean Kiwi. But she is adamant she will always represent New Zealand and remain a New Zealand citizen. GETTY IMAGES

BIG BERTHA

Danyon Loader at the 1996 Olympics in Atlanta. Loader told media after winning two gold medals in the 200 metres and 400 metres freestyle that his goal was to swim a personal best. 'He was trying to beat himself not race others — and if his personal best was good enough then he wins the gold medal,' Hodge says. 'Lydia seems to have clicked on to that at a very early age.'

The other thing Lydia has done is avoid falling into the trap of seeking perfection.

Perfectionism, in the psychological sense, has been broadly defined as striving for exceedingly high standards, accompanied by harsh self-criticism.

'Perfectionism is often portrayed in a bad light — there's positive perfectionism and negative perfectionism, and Lydia seems to have a healthy dose of positive perfectionism,' Hodge insists.

'Some people get so wound up trying to be perfect that they live their lives in a constant state of stress, because no one can ever be perfect and they can never enjoy it. She seems to have a self-prescribed standard that doesn't allow her to be held to a hundred per cent standard by others.'

For her part, Lydia claims to not 'feel like I'm [a] perfectionist but people say I have that kind of personality'.

The trick for Lydia — and the thing that stops her endlessly pursuing an unattainable ideal — is that while she will do everything she can to create the best possible shot, or outcome, she accepts perfectionism is impossible in the notoriously fickle world of golf.

Golf is Not a Game of Perfect is the title of a seminal golf psychology book by Dr Bob Rotella, an American who has worked with some of the world's top professionals. It's also a phrase John Lister used with little Lydia Ko when showing her the ropes at Gulf Harbour — and it's something she seems to have taken on board in a manner many other players cannot replicate.

'There can never be a perfect round of golf,' Lydia observed. 'Even if you made eighteen birdies, couldn't some of the putts have gone in the middle of the hole instead of the side? Couldn't all the drives have gone in the perfect centre of the fairway? In fact, couldn't you just leave your putter [at] home because every approach shot went in the hole instead of stopping three feet away?'

Understanding that she's human, rather than a robot, and not expecting impossible standards of herself has ensured Lydia doesn't mentally torture herself by seeking a Holy Grail that simply does not exist.

The flipside of not expecting absolute perfection is to accept that mistakes are going to happen, and when they do, Lydia reacts without the emotion of negative self-assessment.

'Golf is infuriatingly difficult,' Hodge observes, 'but when you watch Lydia, if she hits a poor shot and the camera zooms in on her face she will have this quizzical look which says, "Hmm, what happened there?" Other players frequently show some sort of anger, emotion or frustration about what went wrong, but for her it's: "What happened there and how can I fix it?"'

No matter how well you're playing golf, you will get quirky bounces, or the wind will pick up as you hit your shot, or a camera will click during your backswing — a myriad of things can cause a bad shot or an unfortunate bounce. Unless a player can get their head around the minefields that lurk in the psychological landscape of golf, it will create stress and anxiety which Hodge says 'no sane human being can cope with'.

'The way to prevent that catastrophic thinking leaking into your consciousness is to be able to create that forgiving mindset that says "stuff is going to happen that I can't control" — for someone so young to have sorted that out is quite remarkable.'

Lydia's way of dealing with mistakes, her way of forgiving herself, is to laugh. 'When I laugh after making a bogey, it's not because I think bogeys are funny. What I'm laughing at is how clumsy I was to hit a shot that led to the bogey. You can get angry at yourself for making silly mistakes, or you can laugh. Laughing is better.'

The question is where does this ability come from? Can it be trained? Or is it innate?

If it can be trained, surely every player would have the same serene aura as Lydia — and we know that's not the case.

Hodge says the science is far from conclusive, but in his view top athletes can be born with certain skills that are moulded by their environment.

'I would agree there are genetic components as to how people think, but studies of twins have shown that people with identical DNA can grow up to be different people even though they've grown up in the same family environment. Different things have influenced them and nurtured them in different ways and they've ended up being different people — not better or worse, just different.

'Clearly, Lydia has been born with a special talent, which she's worked extraordinarily hard to polish, but she's had great messages from her coach, her mental skills person and her parents. Golf has a lot of pushy, hothouse parents, but hers have seemed quite grounded. It's a confluence of great, positive influences and she's been mature enough to take on the lessons.'

And there's another key on the ring of greatness: taking on the messages, or rather blocking out the messages that could have derailed her and driven her out of the game, as happened with Michelle Wie.

Somehow Lydia has shut herself off from all the external pressures that come in from a world obsessed with winning. Media, sponsors, friends . . . all are guilty of looking at the scoreboard and assessing performances based on finishing positions. We live in a world where all the messages scream 'win'. It's hard, if not impossible, for athletes to avoid that white noise but Lydia, even as a teenager, has been able to dial into her own frequency. She measures her success by her own standards, which come back to being technically excellent, without seeking unattainable perfection, having fun and enjoying the process without worrying about the outcome.

As if to hammer home the message, Michelle Wie herself, when asked by the *New York Times* if she had a message for Lydia — in essence a message for her younger self — said: 'I would say have fun and try your hardest. It's really a game, after all. And I would just say, just play for yourself. Don't play for anyone else. It's your game, your life and it's your desire.'

And therein lies a difference of sorts, because from a young age Lydia seems to have seen and understood exactly what others spend a lifetime trying to learn.

Having conquered the factors that are associated with burnout, Lydia has also added to her armoury the key weapons needed for the opposite of burnout — what's known as athlete engagement.

Athletes who are engaged with their sport simply want to do more, and not just more training; it's about lifting the intensity of training, looking for new challenges, doing more to help others, aiming higher.

And this comes from within — it's not something that can be forced on an athlete. For Lydia, it's summed up in a moment of self-assessment when she stated she couldn't think of a time when she *didn't* love golf.

Chapter Ten

It's Supergirl

If Lydia didn't know she was a superstar, she got a fair idea of her status in New Zealand when she landed in Christchurch for the 2013 New Zealand Open, which had moved from Pegasus to Clearwater Resort.

A city decorated in promotional material that read 'Ready, Set, Ko' greeted her on arrival.

It's a measure of how keen organisers were to cash in on this booming talent who at 15 carried not only the golfing hopes of the nation — after all, no New Zealander had actually won the New Zealand Open — but had a hand in driving revenue as well.

Lydia also seemed caught up in the hype, professing that she wanted to match her performance in other countries by improving on her past performances in her home country. 'I've never performed as well as I wanted here,' she said on arrival.

Talk about marking yourself hard! Given she'd played three New Zealand Opens as a 12-, 13- and 14-year-old and had had two top-10 finishes, her play had been exemplary, but the stakes — and her standards — had risen with the win in Canada.

Perhaps she did actually feel some pressure to deliver. Just as she had after winning the US Amateur, she burst into tears as she held off American Amelia Lewis to score a heart-stopping one-shot win to claim her first New Zealand Open title and her third professional win.

Amid the tears and congratulatory hugs, Lydia, without a hint of teenage blush, admitted a certain rugby player had caught her eye. All Blacks and Crusaders star Israel Dagg, normally the one asked for pictures, queued up to get a photo with Lydia after her win. 'That guy that asked for a picture, he was good-looking. Really good-looking,' she blurted in a refreshingly teenage way.

Their paths would soon cross again in different circumstances but, for now, Dagg was just another in a line of admirers for a youngster whose three professional tournament wins as an amateur were a feat unparalleled in the modern game.

As Fairfax writer Fred Woodcock noted: 'A golf official was overheard to say the only person who could top her achievements as an amateur is Bobby Jones, winner of 13 major championships, including a grand slam in 1930.'

Jones, the founder of Augusta National, was the best amateur golfer of his era only because his wealth meant he did not have to worry about sullying himself with the thought of playing for cash.

'The key point [the official] was making, I think,' continued Woodcock, 'is that she's achieved more than the great Tiger

Woods as an amateur.'

By now Lydia was amateur only in the fact she went home with her wallet empty. In every other sense she was as professional as they come; in fact, throughout 2013 she didn't play any amateur events and never turned out again for her country. She had conquered all frontiers in the amateur ranks and had no need to retrace her steps at a lower tier.

Any doubts about her growing A-list status were dispelled when she took up an invitation to play at the New Zealand PGA, a pro-am event where professional golfers play alongside amateurs and celebrities. Lydia found herself at home, casually rubbing shoulders with the likes of New Zealand prime minister John Key and Hollywood actor Don Cheadle.

'It's not often that you get to play alongside a Hollywood star, give golf tips to the prime minister, and take on the top male pros,' she said, as if such behaviour was, in fact, an everyday occurrence in her newly minted superstar life. She struck up such a rapport with Cheadle, the pair later traded Twitter messages and went out for dinner before a tournament in America.

After the fun, Lydia hit the road to play professional tournaments around the world, from Hawaii to New York, Japan, Scotland, Canada and France. And in every single one of them she made the cut, the halfway mark in a professional event where the top 60 or so players are separated from the also-rans who go home empty-handed.

By the time she turned 16 in April, she had made the cut in 16 successive professional events and put herself increasingly in the mix for trophies — if not cash.

In June, she equalled her best performance in a major championship, tying for 17th at the LPGA Championship, six shots adrift of Inbee Park.

A month later she tied for 36th at the US Open in New York after carding an even par 72 in the final round. But — shock, horror — she didn't win the leading amateur honours, which went to American Casie Cathrea.

Inbee Park again took the title, creating history by winning the first three major championships of the year, only the second player in the history of the LPGA Tour to achieve that treble and the first in the modern era.

Inbee was the pacesetter for women's golf and for Lydia she represented yet another older Korean to hunt down as she had done with Cecilia Cho and Sharon Ahn.

Horrendous weather is a fact of life on Britain's famous links courses, exposed as they are to coastal winds and lashing rain. The weather that pummelled the Women's British Open, played at the 'home of golf', St Andrews in Scotland, sparked the first, and perhaps only, record of Lydia showing even the slightest hint of annoyance over bad luck.

Golfers often talk about getting on the 'wrong side of the draw' at a golf event. This happens at events like major championships where the time between the first tee-off and last hole-out during the opening two rounds can be well over 12 hours and as much as 15 hours at a course like St Andrews, where all the players start on the first tee rather than being split to start off the first and 10th tees to speed up play.

On such drawn-out days, the weather can change quite dramatically from morning to afternoon and depending when you play in the day, you can cop it worse than others.

At St Andrews in 2013, the weather was both variable and extreme, slapping one half of the field quite hard while gently caressing the other side of the draw.

Those on Lydia's side of the draw endured the worst of the wind on the second afternoon. After a calm morning the wind howled so viciously, play was suspended before she could complete her round. The next morning, she had to go back out in the tail-end of the storm to finish her round while those who went out in the afternoon benefited from an abating breeze.

Lydia remained stoic: 'They [the organisers] did what they thought was the right thing and I can't really complain because others were experiencing it too.'

Her six-over par total earned her a share of the leading amateur prize, alongside England's Georgia Hall, 14 shots back from the winner Stacy Lewis, who won by two strokes.

In August, Lydia returned to Canada to defend her maiden LPGA title and after the first day hinted that the hectic travel schedule had taken its toll.

'When I tried to wake up this morning my eyelids weren't coming up,' she said in her post-round press conference. 'I said, "Oh, my God, I'm just tired."'

Tired or not, Lydia tore around the Royal Mayfair Golf Club in Edmonton to claim a share of the round-one lead with American Angela Stanford and told journalists she felt the pressure of playing for a 'double miracle' after her win the previous year.

The pressure, though, came entirely from within — as defending champion Lydia felt she had to deliver to a higher standard than normal. It was an unusual feeling for her in that she felt obliged to live up to others' hype. Seeking some counsel for how she was feeling, she called her dad, who wisely told her: 'Relax, you can't control everything, and just play the game that you want to play and that you planned.'

Three days later, her plan executed to perfection, Lydia became the first player to successfully defend a title on the

LPGA Tour since former world number one Yani Tseng claimed back-to-back British Opens in 2010 and 2011.

Amid the adulation, astonishment and awe-struck search for adjectives, journalists were left rolling in the aisle at her press conference as Lydia found a way to disarm them with her self-deprecating humour — confessing she couldn't enjoy the celebratory walk up the 18th fairway despite a massive lead.

'I don't know why, but especially when there are a lot of people, I kind of forget how to walk,' she said to raucous laughter at her press conference. 'Because you walk without thinking, but today I was like, oh, my gosh, right foot forward, left foot forward . . . I wasn't feeling like myself. So I was like, oh, my God, am I walking weird?'

As an analogy for how to play golf it was perfect — the more you think about it the harder it gets, something Lydia recognised herself: 'When you are right there in the moment you don't really know what you are doing, you just go with the flow,' she said.

Her final round 64 in Montreal gave her a five-shot win. She became the first amateur and the youngest player to win twice on the LPGA Tour.

Again the professionals were amazed at their young rival. 'Lydia pretty much whipped all of us today! Congrats,' Suzann Pettersen tweeted after the round. Caroline Hedwall, the third-round leader left in Lydia's wake, said: 'Lydia just went off. She was unbelievable today.'

Coach Guy Wilson watched each shot of the final round from his home in Auckland and noted what the world now understands: when Lydia's sometimes mercurial putting stroke is dialled in no one can stop her. She is so accurate off the tee, seldom misses the green — and if the flatstick is working like a wand, she will invariably be around the top of the leaderboard.

As an amateur Lydia once again missed out on a massive pay day, prompting Claude Mongeau of tournament sponsor CN (Canadian National Railway) to quip after the event that Lydia was a 'dream for a sponsor — she doesn't even pick up the cheque!'

By now Lydia had forfeited more than NZ$1 million in unclaimed cheques, but she insisted it was no big deal.

'I know I'm not going to get the money, so I don't really care. I don't care. I don't care. I can say that a couple times more, if you want.'

However, the natural question — the inevitable question — soon followed: when would she care enough to turn professional?

'I've got some people above me — my mum and dad — they're the boss and they're going to help me make the right decision to turn pro. As I'm only sixteen, it's quite hard to make huge decisions. When I turn pro it's like a job, it's all about money — my parents, New Zealand Golf, Institute of Golf will all have a say.'

Publicly, the plan, despite success rolling in like waves, hadn't changed. Team Ko just had to close their minds to the money, knowing there would be plenty more where that came from once she did turn professional. But behind closed doors, they were feverishly reassessing the idea of having to wait another two years to play for cash.

The other persistent note in the background was whether Lydia could become the youngest ever winner of a major championship. Morgan Pressel, of the United States, held the women's record, being 18 years, 10 months, 9 days when she won the 2007 Kraft Nabisco Championship.

The men's record holder, Young Tom Morris, was just 17 when he won his first British Open in 1868, but he belonged to a completely different era of golf. If Lydia won a tournament

Lydia Ko's results in professional events in 2013 (as an amateur)

(T = tied)

1st — New Zealand Women's Open

2nd — New South Wales Open

3rd — Australian Open

T4th — JLPGA (LPGA of Japan Tour) World Ladies' Championship Salonpas Cup

T9th — LOTTE LPGA Championship, Hawaii

T14th — Thailand PGA (LPGA Tour event)

T25th and leading amateur — Kraft Nabisco (major)

T17th — LPGA Championship (major)

T4th — Walmart NW Arkansas Championship

T36th — US Open Championship (major)

T7th — Marathon Classic (LPGA Tour)

T42nd and joint leading amateur — British Open (major)

1st — Canadian Open (first amateur to win back to back)

2nd — Evian Championship (major) (leading amateur)

at a younger age than Young Tom she would become an instant golfing immortal.

Both those marks were in Lydia's sights when in September she went into the final day of the Evian Championship in southwest France tied for the lead with Suzann Pettersen of Norway.

There's a reason Young Tom Morris is likely to forever have his name cast in stone — winning a major championship is damn hard. In the final round Lydia, despite a great performance, fell two shots shy of Pettersen, shooting 70 to the older woman's 68 to finish runner-up.

'I tried to play my own game, set my own goals,' said Ko. 'If somebody else played better, like Suzann did today, I can't do anything about it.'

Unlike in Canada, Lydia didn't have her best day on greens. It was one of those rounds where her putting stroke was just slightly off and she lost confidence in this most delicate area of the game. Her performance wasn't helped by the greens being slightly bumpy as a result of renovations carried out earlier in the year and a biblical deluge of rain on the first day, which played havoc with the reworked surfaces.

It was the same for all players and Lydia didn't blame the greens, but the fact is Suzann Pettersen was twice her age and had vastly more experience of handling trying conditions. Sometimes youth has drawbacks.

The tournament ended a draining run of demanding events, including all five majors, and without a missed cut. Unsurprisingly, Lydia's last words on the Evian Championship were: 'I miss home.'

Rather bizarrely, Lydia arrived home to the kind of fanfare last seen in New Zealand when Michael Campbell won the US

Open in 2005, including a full-on press conference at Auckland Airport where coach Guy Wilson sat alongside her and fielded questions.

As they had through their 10-year relationship, Guy and Lydia traded banter and jokes, poking fun at the media's obsession with when she'd turn pro while at the same time suggesting the move was closer than they'd previously indicated.

In hindsight, their informal ease and almost comedic back and forth had a pinch of poignancy. It looked to all the world as if the pair were about to embark on a new career step together.

But only one of them would go on to the big show.

Chapter Eleven

End of an era, start of a reign

The video skit Lydia put on with All Blacks star Israel Dagg to announce her new life as a professional in October 2013 stunned the world for its humour, cleverness, high production values and quintessential Generation Zero approach. And it was . . . fun.

Lyds and Izzy hooning around Gulf Harbour in a golf cart, Lydia the straight woman to Dagg's enthusiastic funny man — jumping around like a puppy in a bunker he badgers her about when she's going to turn pro before saying, 'Well, if you can beat me you can definitely handle the pressure of going pro.

Must be time now.'

'OK, I'll do it,' Lydia says, so low-key it's like she's been told to tidy her room.

And with that, the best amateur golfer of her generation sent a shudder through the play-for-pay ranks: Lydia Ko was turning pro.

The announcement broke all the rules of how you're supposed to do these things, but Lydia had been rearranging furniture in the golf world all her life, so why break with that?

Why do a boring old press conference in front of a few Kiwi journalists when you can make a YouTube video seen by hundreds of thousands of people around the globe? Why sit and take questions out of your control when you can make and manage your own content and deliver the message as a modern teenager should? Like her golf, Lydia's announcement was about doing things her way and controlling the controllables.

Lydia later revealed she'd wanted to do something 'out of the ordinary' to announce her decision to join the paid ranks, but she also wanted to avoid the fuss and carry-on involved in a press conference as she hunkered down to prepare for end-of-year exams.

The video served a dual purpose for New Zealand Golf as both Lydia and Dagg were ambassadors of a new promotion — Love Golf — designed to boost the game's flagging popularity in New Zealand and dispel a few myths about it being the domain of crusty, aloof and grumpy old men.

However, with the announcement Lydia now faced a problem: the LPGA Tour had a minimum age requirement of 18 — and her 18th birthday was 18 months away.

So just as Team Ko did in lobbying Pupuke Golf Club for an early membership, they set about lobbying the LPGA to waive the rules.

LPGA Commissioner Michael Whan might have given the appearance of taking a couple of days to mull over the decision before making a suitably plain statement to the effect Lydia had been granted permission to start her career in the 2014 season.

The truth is the LPGA Tour needed Lydia as much as she needed it. When Whan took over the reins of the tour in 2010, it wasn't exactly struggling but it was bearing the brunt of the global financial crisis, had difficulty getting its events on TV and had a perception problem in America: there were too many foreigners who didn't speak English, which therefore made it hard for fans to appreciate and sponsors to leverage. In fact, the tour struggled to host a full schedule of events, with the calendar totalling just 22 tournaments.

Whan dedicated himself to making the sponsors happy. And nothing makes sponsors happier than a delightful teen prodigy hell-bent on rewriting history. Plus, she had charisma and charm.

The fact Lydia had already won two Canadian Opens and was No. 5 in the world also had a bearing on Whan's decision. It would have been churlish to keep the door shut on such a star — in reality, they couldn't unlock it fast enough.

When Lydia finally did front for a press conference, journalists asked what she'd do with her first cheque as a professional.

'I guess I will have to think about that with my parents because I am still sixteen. Just because I am turning pro doesn't mean that I can do everything my way.'

Questions around Guy Wilson's future were raised as rumours swirled of a split but Lydia expertly sidestepped them, neither confirming nor denying her future with Wilson. But in hindsight, and reading between the lines, the death knell for the coach–player relationship had been signalled.

Lydia's first assignment as a professional was the LPGA's season-ending event, reserved for players crowned champions during the year, held in 2013 at Tiburon Golf Club in Florida. She took her place in this CME Group Titleholders tournament thanks to the Canadian Open victory, and in an ultra-consistent but not outstanding performance finished in a tie for 21st and a first pay day of NZ$20,000.

Asked what she'd do with her first pay, Lydia said she planned to buy a camera at her next venue, Taiwan, to start documenting her first year as a professional. Photography had been one of her favourite subjects at school and she wanted to make sure she kept at it, especially to keep her from over-focusing on golf.

'The better the results, hopefully the better the equipment I can get, right?' she joked. By the time she left Taiwan she would be able to afford any camera she liked.

Lydia headed to Taiwan glowing in the spotlight of being named one of the 16 most influential teenagers in the world by *Time* magazine.

Named alongside her was another 16-year-old from Auckland's North Shore, singer Lorde, thanks to her single 'Royals'. The two young New Zealanders joined Malala Yousafzai, 16, the Pakistani who was shot for standing up for education of girls under Taliban rule; Malia Obama, 15, one of President Barack Obama's daughters; and pop singer Justin Bieber, 19.

It wouldn't be the last time Lydia appeared on one of the influential magazine's lists.

The event in Taiwan in early December, Lydia's last event for 2013 before packing it up for Christmas, was the curiously named Swinging Skirts World Ladies Masters at the Linkou Miramar Golf Country Club.

As a new crowd of golf fans tuned into Lydia's life, the name Swinging Skirts created some discomfort for many who inferred the tournament to be sexist and the name inappropriate. Maybe so, but Swinging Skirts is a Taiwanese non-profit organisation dedicated to growing women's golf and members try to reflect the game's Scottish history by wearing kilts or colourful skirts.

In terms of growing the game, they struck gold when Lydia Ko made their event her first professional triumph.

A final round of three-under-par 69 propelled her past Korean superstars So Yeon Ryu and world No. 1 Inbee Park to win the US$1 million tournament. She took home US$150,000 (NZ$181,000).

'This really is the beginning of a whole new era,' said Australian television commentator Sandra Mackenzie-Wood.

Lydia, though, remained low-key as she accepted her trophy and prizemoney — a new era may have dawned, but for Lydia it was just one more step on the ladder of success.

Guy Wilson was blown away by his young prodigy's composure, stating publically how proud he was of her performance and that she had proved she was a player of the future.

But within just a few days, it was announced that Wilson's future with Lydia was over.

'Teenage star Lydia Ko has split with the only golf coach she's ever had, a risky move given the hugely successful partnership,' read the news reports as the end of the decade-long partnership between Lydia and Wilson was revealed.

The official line on the coaching split was that Lydia's increased time overseas coupled with Wilson staying in New Zealand meant parting ways was inevitable.

Lydia said the split was 'definitely not an easy decision' but in subsequent interviews hinted there was more than one factor behind the change.

Wilson, while noting his 'incredible disappointment' and touching on how close he'd become to the Ko family, was magnanimous in his short statement, saying it had been an

Guy Wilson's legacy will always be as the person who recognised Lydia's genius well before anyone else and had the nous to turn that potential into an exceptional golfer.

honour to develop Lydia into the No. 4 golfer in the world and wishing her the best in a career he would watch with pride.

Others, though, were not quite so restrained about the split.

Michael Hendry, a leading New Zealand professional and Lydia's stablemate at the Institute of Golf, voiced the loudest dissent, saying: 'Isn't it amazing how big business and big money can make people forget who really cares about them?'

The implication was that a deal Lydia had signed with global marketing giant International Management Group (IMG) was behind the decision to dump Wilson in favour of IMG-linked coach David Leadbetter.

Many felt Wilson had been treated badly, that he'd been used and jettisoned just as he was set to benefit the most from Lydia's money-earning potential. His silence on the matter only increased his standing in the golf community. His legacy will always be as the person who recognised Lydia's genius well before anyone else and had the nous to turn that potential into an exceptional golfer. His personality was an important influence on how Lydia approaches the game and to this day he's still an influence on how she conducts herself on a golf course.

But the truth was that Lydia had been casting around for other coaches for some time and the feeling in the Ko camp was that Wilson had taken Lydia as far as possible and now fresh eyes were needed.

Whatever the reasons for the split, it was — in many ways — typical of the way Lydia had progressed through life, always seeking to challenge herself, to adapt and innovate. Changing her coach was bound to be part of that at some stage.

Other critics echoed Hendry's sentiments about the power of IMG to unduly influence Lydia's outlook on life. The biggest fear was that IMG would try to leverage her for everything she was worth — and that she was worth more flying a Korean flag.

This echoed the oft-quoted reservation about the influx of Korean golfers into New Zealand, namely the fear they would use everything on offer in New Zealand, including taxpayer assistance, to develop their game before high-tailing back to Korea to cash in on their success. It had happened with Sharon Ahn, Cecilia Cho and other less high-profile players so it was a natural response.

But Lydia stayed constantly firm on her decision she would remain a New Zealander.

'I've been playing for New Zealand the last couple of years, and I haven't made any plans to change it at all,' she said at the time. 'I love it here, the culture and the country itself.'

IMG, faced with criticism of steering the youngster in the wrong direction, were adamant they would take a 'back seat' in her golf career, cleverly noting 'her family [was] still very much running the show'.

As they'd done since Lydia was five, Gil Hong and Tina would continue to drive things on the practical side. Her father would still have an influence on coaching and her mother would manage her day-to-day life, a tight circle that would soon include Lydia's sister Sura, who joined IMG to become one of Lydia's official managers. This decision seems to indicate it was the Ko family driving IMG decisions and not the other way around. While the family handled golf-related matters, IMG looked after marketing and sponsorship.

For a giant company with the clout of IMG to say they were 'perfectly happy to be in the background' says much for the ultra-professional way the Ko clan were already running Lydia's career.

As for the coaching side of things, it was later revealed Lydia would work with Florida-based Sean Hogan, originally from

Dublin, Ireland, and one of the coaches at David Leadbetter's academy.

Lydia had previously met David Leadbetter after taking advice from Leadbetter student Suzann Pettersen, who had edged her at the Evian Championship.

'I decided to try it and it felt really good,' she said of a session with Leadbetter. 'Guy has been a great coach and great friend and [it's] sad to say goodbye but there are processes that had to happen.'

Copping flak from all directions on how she closed the chapter on one of the most important facets of her life definitely hurt Lydia, say those who are close to her, and it wasn't the only controversy she courted as she transitioned from amateur to professional, with — not surprisingly — money being at the heart of things.

One of the things that is said to have most upset Lydia in her final year as an amateur was the perception she milked the public purse in taking funding from the taxpayer-fed High Performance Sport New Zealand (HPSNZ).

Golf came into the Olympic cycle leading up to the Rio games (from 2013 to 2016) and therefore Lydia earned a personal grant of $185,000 in both 2013–14 and 2014–15. The grants caused confusion on two levels: the first was that the money was to help prepare for a professional career, and the second concern was that she was taking money from taxpayers when, having turned professional, she was more than capable of paying her own way.

High Performance Sport was forced to clarify what it called 'misinformation' in the media over the Olympic funding.

First, the money was designed to prepare her for the Rio

Olympics, not to enable her to transition to the pro ranks. Second, New Zealand Golf's application for two years' worth of funding for Lydia came in 2012 when she was still an amateur and was expected to remain an amateur for the two years covered by the funding period.

High Performance Sport chief executive Alex Baumann said the funding was justified because Lydia had the potential to win a medal for New Zealand at the Olympic Games and that even though she had turned professional his organisation had a role to play in ensuring she was a genuine gold medal chance at Rio.

Nevertheless, Lydia and New Zealand Golf — noting their disappointment at the media coverage — felt like they'd been painted into a corner and between them decided, in May 2014, to turn down the funding slated for the 2014–15 financial year.

Unreported at the time was the fact Lydia actually paid back some money already awarded to her and which overlapped her professional career.

Lydia is a New Zealand citizen and has made a very public commitment to her adopted country. While she'd become a New Zealander, however, Korea took great pride in what she had achieved — too much pride, it turned out.

Many organisations and individuals wanted to help cover the expenses the Kos incurred in creating their daughter's dream through the trust fund New Zealand Golf was running. But for reasons that have never fully been explained, the Korean Development Bank — a Korean government-owned bank — tried give more than $100,000 to Tina and Gil Hong by channelling it through the Auckland Korean Society.

There was nothing wrong with the donation per se, but in taking the money, the Korean Society, a charitable organisation, broke its own rules, sparking an investigation by the Department of Internal Affairs.

It was enough to drive headlines — after all, the keywords were perfect: superstar golfer, broken rules, money, investigation — and it played out over a number of days in the media.

Moving money through the accounts of the Korean Society was a naive move which the bank tried to justify by saying it wanted to hide the money so it wouldn't be seen as backing a non-Korean citizen.

Then there were the repercussions, with police being called to a subsequent meeting of the Korean Society, which got out of hand as accusations were flung around the room as to who was responsible for this black mark against the organisation and against Lydia's good name.

A third day of headlines followed when Gil Hong Ko announced he was going to sue certain members of the Auckland Korean Society for bringing Lydia's name into disrepute.

In the end, the punishment for 'deliberately concealing' the money was a slap on the wrist for the Korean Society, but the repercussions of the unseemly and unnecessary scandal were to raise questions over whether Lydia had breached her amateur status, which she hadn't.

It's estimated Lydia needed close to $200,000 towards the end of her amateur career when she was almost constantly overseas, nearly all of which came from the trust fund administered by New Zealand Golf, which ensured all legitimate expenses were paid retrospectively.

The biggest — or most public — backer of the trust was businessman Sir David Levene.

The man who built and sold the Levenes empire played his golf at Gulf Harbour where Lydia was a member.

'I'm just so proud of the kid — she's an absolutely lovely little person,' Sir David said in a rare interview with the *New Zealand Herald* about his support for her. 'I was so chuffed when she won the Canadian Open but I've been chuffed with everything she has done . . .

'If she can keep her present plans going forward as an amateur for a few years I have every hope she'll be a very successful professional and make her life in golf.'

Once she turned professional, Lydia's major backer — apart from golf club manufacturer Callaway — was ANZ Bank, whose logo features prominently on her playing shirt. The bank signed Lydia to a three-year deal when she turned pro.

All the money matters were handled by her family, with the money-go-round bypassing Lydia.

'I try and concentrate on my game. If they send me clothes with logos, I'll wear them. I'm wearing what I need to be wearing. Those business aspects, that's what my parents do and IMG does. It's kind of really good that I don't need that to think about. It's hard enough just being able to get that ball in the hole.'

Being Lydia, she would say that — but getting the little white ball in the hole came more naturally to her than many.

Chapter Twelve

A swing of beauty

'Hypnotically robotic, thoroughly repeatable and extremely beautiful.' That's how golf writer Michael Bamberger described Si Re Pak's golf swing in 1998.

Almost twenty years later, Lydia Ko's former amateur teammate Emily Perry echoed those words in describing Lydia's swing: 'Robotic but beautifully robotic — there's not another word for it.'

Great golf swings come in as many forms and shapes as there are players. For some it comes naturally, for others it's like trying to drink a cup of tea while brushing their hair.

In the 1960s and 70s the best male players of the era, Jack Nicklaus, Arnold Palmer, Tom Watson and Lee Trevino, had four quite diverse and unique swings.

In the modern era we've seen recent Masters tournaments at Augusta won by the likes of Bubba Watson, Adam Scott and Jordan Spieth, who would be at three corners of a triangle when it comes to swing differences.

Scott is pure class, his technique as neat and orderly as his dress sense; Watson won two Masters with his homemade, all-arms-and-legs swing which created immense power and sent the ball arcing through the air like it was a cyclist banking the walls of a velodrome; while Spieth, with his 'chicken wing' left arm, is a prime example of substance over style.

In the women's game the diversity is even more obvious. Inbee Park with her upright, choppy swing gives the appearance of someone who learned golf in a parallel universe to Na Yeon Choi, a Korean on the LPGA Tour whose pretty, rhythmic swing is regarded as one of the most aesthetically pleasing on the planet.

Then there's Michelle Wie with her incredibly flexible, athletic, high-torque swing, and Lexi Thompson with her aggressive body language, almost a female version of Bubba Watson.

What all these swings have in common — what all good golfers have in common — is no matter how they swing the golf club they manage to bring the club face back to the right position, to square the club face as they say in golfing speak. It's the repeatability of a golf swing that is more critical than how it looks.

And Lydia, former coach Guy Wilson has said, had 'the ability to square the club face up like no one. It's pretty freaky, and really, really early you could see it.'

Technically, her mechanics are not perfect; as an amateur she had what some would consider minor flaws. Her club face at the top of the backswing was in a position some swing gurus would call 'wrong' and as a result she had to unwind her hips incredibly fast to get the club face back to that square position.

Those mechanics were not to everyone's liking. New Zealand golfing great Sir Bob Charles was not a fan, once telling a New Zealand Golf AGM that Lydia's swing wouldn't cause him to pause and watch if he passed her on the driving range. Yet he acknowledged there was another facet to Lydia's swing he couldn't ignore . . . an intangible that brings out rich descriptions, such as 'mystical' and 'flawless metronome' . . . it's the *way* she swings the club. Unlike gymnastics or diving, there are no points awarded for artistic merit in golf and yet golf fans crave a swing that is aesthetically pleasing.

With Lydia, it's the way she brings all the moving parts together with a seamless rhythm and a tempo you could set a watch by. There's a languid and relaxed nature to the swing that gives the feel of running water. She never jerks, overextends, gets out of balance or hurls herself at the ball. The club goes back, there's a hint of a pause like that between an inhale and exhale, and then it flows around her body with the silkiness of a cat's tail.

All the while she gives the impression of unhurried grace, her pleasing tempo never changing, no matter what club she is wielding or the pressure of the situation.

Her swing, as they say, was grooved. And when a swing is like that all the advice is not to change.

While Lydia had made subtle changes along the way, adjusting her grip to compensate for the wrist injury she suffered, and constantly making minor alterations as she grew through her teen years, she always managed to bring the variety of moving parts together with an artistry not lost on her new coach David Leadbetter, who described her swing as a 'Mona Lisa'.

Why then did he take a work of art, paint over the top of it and hang it in a new frame? Why did he change Lydia's golf swing so dramatically that critics feared her game would disintegrate and she'd end up injured and on the waste pile?

The first hint Leadbetter was overhauling Lydia's swing drew some stinging critiques.

'The thing that perplexes me about Lydia Ko is that she continues to tweak this golf swing,' said former PGA Tour pro Charlie Rymer, on his regular Golf Channel show. 'When I first saw her golf swing, I really thought it was very close to perfection. The work ethic, constantly trying to improve and get better, that's all great, until you get to the top of the world. Then, I think you've got to shift gears, and rather than continue to change, change, change, you have to learn to repeat, repeat, repeat.'

Rymer believed that Lydia hadn't quite got to that phase yet, and thought it 'scary that she continues to tweak her golf swing. The golf graveyard is full of great players that continued to tweak after they'd already figured it out. I hope she doesn't become one of those tombstones in that graveyard.'

Rymer's co-host, LPGA professional Paige Mackenzie, agreed. 'I'm incredibly perplexed that she's continuing to change. It's scary to be in that much of a different position in your backswing than you were prior. Whenever I see a player move away from what they do naturally, it is a little bit frightening.'

Even PGA Tour star Billy Horschel tweeted: 'She had a beautiful swing before Leadbetter got his hands on it. Super talented player. She's a stud!'

To understand some of this criticism, you have to understand David Leadbetter, who built his reputation on renovating Nick Faldo's swing and turning the Englishman into a golfing genius who won six major championships.

While Faldo's success is the shining beacon, Leadbetter, a South Africa-born Englishman living in America, is also regarded as an eccentric in possession of kooky methods. The term 'Lead poisoning' is used by some in reference to the way he has befuddled some players.

Lydia's arrival at the Leadbetter academy in Florida coincided almost perfectly with the public release of his new book detailing a brazen new teaching method known as the A-Swing, short for Alternative Swing.

For golf fans, the best description of the Leadbetter A-Swing is to say it looks like the swing implemented by Jim Furyk, who has the most distinctively different method on the US PGA Tour, a swing once described by Northern Irish commentator David Feherty as being like 'an octopus falling out of a tree'.

Yet Furyk is a major champion, having won the US Open, and is a perennial contender on the PGA into his forties — and his swing is renowned for its accuracy.

The A-Swing, according to Leadbetter, overturns the best part of 30 years' teaching focused on what is known as the one-plane swing, where players swing the golf club back and forward along the same curved line so the club face traces a nice arc (although this is way oversimplifying it).

The A-Swing, in contrast, sees the clubhead (and again to oversimplify) trace what looks like the ribbon symbol used for AIDS awareness, or a shoelace — up on one track, a loop, then down another track.

It has its rationale. The one-plane swing is hard to execute because it's maddeningly difficult to stay on-plane throughout the swing; you need almost perfect control of legs, hips, torso, spine, shoulders, arms and hands, which are all moving independently.

Instead, if you just take the club back on the shortest possible route and then move it to a new position, all you're really worried about is getting synchronised on the way down, argues Leadbetter, who compares the swing to what a batter does in baseball.

While cynics might see some mileage in Leadbetter using Lydia as a vehicle to showcase his A-Swing to the world, it seems the changes to her swing were actually instigated by her parents, which again shows how much influence they have over her career.

The controversial move to Leadbetter arose, in part, because Gil Hong admired the swing of Hee Young Park, a young Korean who worked with Leadbetter and is now playing on the LGPA Tour.

And Tina, according to Randall Mell of Golf Channel, told Leadbetter she wanted her daughter's swing overhauled because she wanted rid of the 'shut face and have her gain some more distance'.

Removing the 'shut' club face — best described by Lydia herself as having the club in a position at the top of her backswing where she could 'fry an egg on a hot day' — also meant eliminating some excessive wrist manipulation which had already caused one minor injury.

And gaining distance was best achieved by changing Lydia's ball flight from a safe fade (a left-to-right ball flight) to a more aggressive draw (right-to-left), which brings greater distance.

It just so happened the A-Swing would help Lydia do both these things.

Leadbetter, perhaps being diplomatic, initially had reservations about changing Lydia's swing as it would be a case of damned if you do and damned if you don't. 'If she played well, she was supposed to play well. If she played badly, well, then it's, "You guys screwed up,"' he said. 'I went through that before with Nick Faldo. It was, "Who the hell are you to mess up our golden boy?"

'It's always a bit of a risk, but you have to take a little bit of risk in life sometimes.'

Leadbetter claimed his A-Swing would 'shake up' the golf world and overturn conventional teaching methods, so having a star who could prove his point was a blessing.

Among the radical redesigns the A-Swing brings to the game are that hands are placed on the shaft in 'opposition' to each other, completely different to the accepted method of the hands being parallel to each other.

Most important, however, is the upright backswing, which Leadbetter described as a 'blatant challenge of convention' but which he argues is the most efficient and simplest backswing to facilitate what matters most: an on-plane downswing. By taking the swing off course on the way back, putting it on course on the way back down became easier.

Whether Lydia needed the A-Swing to achieve what her parents wanted, or whether she was a useful marketing tool for Leadbetter, is a moot point, but the controversial coach has certainly used her success to justify the changes and sell his theory. 'When watching her swing, pay attention to (and enjoy!) the wonderfully free and "alive" energy of her club as she releases it with a controlled yet abandoned lash into the ball. That's Lydia and The A-Swing at their best.'

Leadbetter said the new swing, combined with a training regime focused on her core strength and making her lower body more stable, as well as equipment 'fine-tuned to the nth degree' by Callaway, all combined to add around 20 metres to her driving distance.

As well as completely changing how Lydia swung the club, Leadbetter also changed her long, languid, hypnotic tempo, making it a 'smidgin quicker'. This slightly quicker, shorter swing was designed to stop Lydia using her hips to spin through the shot. In short, claimed Leadbetter, the new swing relied less on the perfect timing of many moving parts and therefore was more efficient.

'Yet, there are still doubters and so-called experts who think we shouldn't have touched her golf swing at all,' he wrote in a blog in 2015. 'When we started with her, she was only 16. It was very easy to make these subtle changes, which ultimately, in my opinion along with many others, have helped her game to move up to another level. Barring unforeseen circumstances, I believe she'll have an Annika Sörenstam type career.' (Sörenstam is one of the most successful female golfers in history.)

Leadbetter noted that Lydia's swing traits were based on his A-Swing philosophy, which 'most golfers on the planet would benefit greatly by copying'.

'All the while, she has maintained her beautiful rhythm — we certainly haven't touched that — she has more shots in her bag, her three-quarter shots are much easier for her and the biggest thing is that she now fully understands the inner workings of her swing.' This, according to Leadbetter, is what leads to repeatability and consistency.

'In the final analysis, though, the biggest thing is that Lydia really loves the A-Swing material that she's working on, and finds it both easy and comfortable to implement it on the course in the LPGA and other worldwide professional events in which she plays.'

John Lister, Lydia's old mentor from her junior days, believes the Leadbetter method has made Lydia a better ball-striker.

'Most of golf teaching is about getting the plane perfect on the way back but it's what happens on the downswing that matters,' Lister says. 'Lydia is getting to be a better ball-striker than she's ever been.'

Having said all that, while the swing has changed in its structure and the tempo has increased slightly, it still has Lydia's fingerprint: the sense of having all the time in the world. She never looks fast or hurried.

PGA Tour pro Charlie Rymer, for all his concerns about the Leadbetter method, noted that Lydia's rhythm remained her defining characteristic.

'She has a distinctive rhythm . . . we saw that in her press conference — she doesn't get hurried; she thinks about what she's going to say, it comes natural to her. If you look at her personality, her golf swing, how she operates, it's very consistent. If you watch her when she walks from the car park to the clubhouse — she walks at the same pace as she walks on the golf course. That pace permeates her entire life and that is the secret to her consistency.'

As in life, so Lydia is in golf: she never gets rushed and never goes hard at the golf ball. Everything is under control — and there's a lesson there for all golfers: her stock shot is a three-quarter swing and she seldom tries to muscle the ball to gain extra distance. She always swings within herself and in balance.

'In golf you have to fight temptation,' she told *Golf Digest*. 'My max[imum] distance with a 9-iron is 120 yards. I've been in situations where I need 122 yards of carry, and sometimes I'll give it a go and succeed. The problem is when the carry is 123 yards.' Then, she acknowledges, 'the temptation to get that extra yard out of the 9-iron is very strong, but I know I'm too far past the max distance. That's when I choose the 8-iron. That decision sounds obvious, but scaling back is really hard for most golfers. We all want to be a hero and be a little better than we are.'

To contain this temptation, Lydia grips her club slightly lower

Lydia's under-control, in-balance swing allows her to maintain her spine angle, one of the most critical factors in the golf swing.

on the shaft than many players. In physics terms this shortens the length of the lever she's using, making it easier to control. But it also shortens the distance of her shots. It means all her golf shots are totally under control in terms of the energy she uses. By staying in control rather than attacking the ball she's able to keep her head still. An obvious contrast here is the great Tiger Woods, who, obsessed with distance and power, would launch himself at the golf ball, which caused his head to bob, something that has been a constant problem throughout his career.

Most importantly, Lydia's under-control, in-balance swing also allows her to maintain her spine angle, one of the most critical factors in the golf swing. While legs, hips, torso, shoulders and arms are all moving, for a golf swing to be effective and for the club face to make the best impact, using the spine like a central pole around which all else rotates is crucial.

As a result, said swing analyst Paige Mackenzie, Lydia has 'one of the most fundamentally sound golf swings I've seen — the spine angle never changes throughout the swing. From the tailbone to top of head it's one straight line that never varies throughout the golf swing.'

The pro golfer added: 'I've never seen . . . a professional, man or woman, who has such strong fundamentals. She's incredibly disciplined and fundamentally strong in a way I've never seen. She doesn't jump up on her toes, she stays nice and balanced.'

For her part, Lydia was happy with the swing and pleased she made the move to Leadbetter and Sean Hogan, despite the furore it caused initially.

'You know, because I had been playing well when I had my old coach, with Guy, there were a lot of words said when I decided to change coaches to Sean and David. Definitely the swings are different to what I used to get taught.'

Lydia acknowledged it had been a good move.

'I think simple has been the big goal without changing a lot of things, especially because we're playing full-time; it's hard to change a lot of things at once. So David is trying to slowly put things into little places and just, like, as if it's sandpaper, just grind away. I've been really liking the way my swing has transitioned.'

The other aspect of Lydia's game — in terms of mechanics — which makes her successful is her putting.

As we've seen in earlier chapters, there have been times in her career, mostly as an amateur, when missed putts from close range have proved costly.

Putting is the part of the game that torments most players, male or female, amateur or professional. The complexities of putting — gauging the slope of a green, the distance the ball will roll, how the type of grass and its grain can affect the roll, bumps, even wind — require an intangible mix of analysis and feel. Overlaying all this is the pressure of putting for tournament wins worth hundreds of thousands of dollars — it's the kind of tension that can turn a gentle touch into a jerky prod.

Then a player must consider techniques, such as cross-handed or normal grip, arc or square stroke, as well as types of putters — short or long, normal handle or fat, heavy or light, blade or mallet, face-weighted or toe-weighted.

Some golfers use the same putter year after year, relying on a trusted friend to do the job without fail, while others are in a never-ending search for just the right club. In the early part of the twenty-first century in men's golf, the two best players in the world were Tiger Woods, who used the same putter year on year, and Vijay Singh, who tried a new putter every other week.

Lydia, for now, falls into the Singh camp, trying all sorts of different putter types, looking for just the right one. And to further complicate things she uses a combination of the two most popular styles of putting, cross-handed and conventional.

Conventional, for a right-hander, means the right hand is below the left. Cross-handed puts the left below the right, which many players use to stop their dominant right hand creating too much movement.

Lydia uses both methods: conventional style for longer putts where the right hand can deliver more force, and cross-handed for close-range putts where she wants more control, using the back of the left hand to guide the club.

According to the statistics on the LPGA Tour, whatever she's doing, it's working. In her rookie year on the tour she was second to Stacy Lewis in the category known as putts per green in regulation, a measure of how many putts on average she takes if she hits the green from the fairway.

Lydia has never believed in superstitions or lucky charms, but when it comes to putting she possesses one habit or routine which she goes through every time. Before she takes a putt of any length she goes to caddy Jason Hamilton (who came on board at the end of 2014) to wipe her hands on a towel he is carrying. At one end of the psychological scale it could be called a tic, at the other end it's a physical cue to get her in the right mental framework to execute the high-pressure shots that decide where the money goes.

The A-Swing or her putting style, however, are not what makes Lydia Ko so good. Plenty of other players have great tempo and rigid spine angles in their swing and many more are great putters under pressure. What Lydia has that sets her apart from so many contenders is an ability to implement her technique in the same way, at the same pace, shot after shot, no matter what is at stake.

As John Lister says, 'technique is minuscule compared to the mental side of it. Will your technique stand up under pressure?'

In the novel *Golf in the Kingdom* by Michael Murphy, the mystical, meditating golf professional Shivas Irons advises his student to 'let the nothingness into your swing'.

It's a philosophy Lydia tries to put into practice.

Asked what she thinks about as she prepares to make a swing, Lydia stated: 'Sometimes when I am in a pressure situation I can get overcomplicated or overthink it so I try not to think about anything — sometimes it's hard to think about not-thinking but that's my swing thought.'

The question we all want to know the answer to is: how do you think about nothing?

Chapter Thirteen

Mind games

For a professional golfer to execute a shot under pressure she needs to separate herself from everything going on around her — the crowd, the money at stake, the mistake she made on the last hole, the state of the contest — as well as closing down the constant stream of chatter the average mind generates, from nonsense such as what's for dinner to greater questions of self-doubt or guilt.

Controlling her mind is one of Lydia Ko's great strengths, from blocking out the effects of pressure, to picturing the type of shots she wants to create, to focusing on the process of the golf swing rather than the result, to pushing emotion to one side and observing her actions from a neutral position, to switching off between shots . . . Lydia seems to have mastered all the psychological techniques regarded as essential for top golf. Her commitment to understanding the mental side of the game is reflected in the fact she has committed to studying psychology by correspondence through Seoul's Korea University.

Her mind-conditioning coach, David Niethe, says she has the mental make-up of all top athletes.

'What we find with great athletes is that balance between the creative mind and the intellectual ability — Lydia has got that in abundance. She is very analytical, very intelligent, but she's got this creative side. When you can blend that together it's something special; she has an incredible mind.'

Niethe is a strong man — a powerlifter — but throughout his sporting career he grew more interested in the strength of the mind. So much so, he changed careers mid-life and went from being a printer to a student of the mind. Curious about creating a mental edge in his own sport, he practised self-hypnosis with 'amazing results' and proceeded to dive head-first into sports psychology. He has worked with top-class swimmers, boxers, mixed martial arts fighters, rugby league players, the New Zealand Breakers basketball team and golfers.

When Lydia first came into his office, at the back of his property in Waterview, Auckland, she was so small 'her feet didn't touch the ground when she sat on the couch'.

Niethe helped hone Lydia's mind from a young age to a razor sharpness which matched her wedge play. The key areas Niethe worked on can be summarised as visualisation, perception and the physiology of excellence. Like her lessons with Guy Wilson, fun featured highly.

'The first fifteen minutes of any session with Lydia was her saying hello to the cats and the dogs. And if you were sitting outside listening to us you'd be wondering if we were doing any work because we'd be cracking up laughing.

'That's how she liked to learn — her learning state was fun. If you made it fun she'd take it all on board. The moment you started getting serious she would actually manipulate it back to fun. She's highly intelligent in that way, in understanding what works for her — she had a level of self-awareness from a very young age. She definitely had a certain level of wisdom and was smart enough to filter out the bullshit.'

Evidence of her desire — and ability — to have fun came at an early age when she could be seen skipping down fairways and picking flowers. In her younger days she copped a bit of flak from other kids and from older members at the Pupuke Golf Club for her joyous romps.

The scowls and sniggers upset the young Lydia but, says Niethe, she was 'congruent' with having fun. In other words, Lydia expressed to the world who she truly was.

Unfazed by what others thought of her, Lydia kept playing golf in a cocoon of fun. For her, enjoyment was the main priority, rather than placing demands on herself to perform.

'She was ultimately at peace with herself and the world around. There was no conflict.'

In terms of visualisation, Niethe worked with Lydia on a number of levels.

Just as the late boxing legend Muhammad Ali once quipped, 'I am the greatest. I said that even before I was', so Niethe had Lydia visualising herself as the world No. 1. In his words it was 'giving herself permission' to be the best and then acting as if that was going to play out as she envisaged.

On a more mundane level, he also taught her to visualise golf shots; to create in her mind's eye the type of golf shot she wanted to play, or to imagine a creative solution to a tricky chip shot or convoluted putt. It relates to his mantra: 'what you think is what you get'.

But there was also a third way of thinking: Lydia's mind examining the outcomes of shots.

Here Niethe and Lydia talked about 'perceptional positioning', a neurolinguistic programming (NLP) term which relates to how we see the world — from our own position, from someone else's position (the old 'walk a mile in someone else's shoes') and from the position of a neutral observer. It's in this third position where we can analyse a situation without any emotion; in Lydia's case, the examination of her golf shot without blaming herself if something went wrong.

Regular golf watchers — and players — will frequently see the opposite of this: players yelling at themselves, calling themselves names, shaking their heads, throwing clubs, blaming caddies. That's the norm, so for Lydia to be able assess a situation without any anger or remorse takes a huge amount of mental skill.

'She learned that she could debrief in a way that didn't affect her self-image,' Niethe says. 'She would dissociate from the emotion and look at the mistakes she made from a neutral position in order to take the learnings but not the emotion. This is not easy stuff — these were advanced techniques that I'd deploy with a young lady who got it.'

You can see this when the camera zooms in to Lydia's face after she's played a shot that doesn't quite come off. The look on her face may be confused or quizzical as she ponders what went wrong technically — or even assessing what went right — and she does this without bringing any negative emotion to the equation.

'And that's the difference,' says Niethe. 'Too many golfers spend more time beating themselves up than getting into a state that helps produce quality shots.

'I talk about the self-image being like a pitcher of water that you hold in front you — it's very vulnerable and every time we have a negative thought, while it seems insignificant, over time it stains the whole thing. If you can go out and be mindful of that, protect that, you will always see where you're going, always have clear direction, always have focus — it's teaching people to become conscious.

'There are a lot of golfers out there who are in constant flight-or-fight mode — they're angry with themselves and it's a constant battle. It should be about becoming at peace with yourself.'

Emily Perry, Lydia's teammate in New Zealand amateur teams who is now studying psychology, saw first hand how Lydia managed to 'navigate this game that can drive you crazy'.

'Golf messes with you. It brings out your insecurities and any negative emotions you have about yourself. I really believe who you are as a person comes out when you play golf. You can't hide from yourself; the game exposes you,' Emily says. 'But it doesn't seem to mess with Lydia — from how she plays a hole, a round, how she sees out a tournament, how she survives on a tour . . .

'I've been on the second-tier tour in Europe and on tour in Australia and everyone drives themselves insane because it's just so hard not to reflect on your negatives or to beat yourself up when things aren't going well, but Lydia doesn't even seem to have that available to her.

'With her she didn't seem to have any negative mental things to pull against. Others of us have bad negative things in life or in tournaments but she seems to have missed that out. Mentally, she doesn't have anything bad to draw on — her pattern is overwhelmingly positive.'

Lydia's positive outlook — simplistically you could quote from the film *Life of Brian* and say she had a way to 'always look on the bright side of life' — is linked to her ability to 'reframe' situations.

Lydia does suffer from nerves and stress like the rest of the world's golfers, but she is better able to handle her physiological reaction to stress.

If she hits a dud shot and it goes behind a tree, she won't fall into the woe-is-me, life-is-unfair trap. Instead she will say to herself: here's an opportunity to create something.

'She just had that ability . . . There's no such thing as a stressful situation, just a new challenge,' says Niethe. 'What an amazing way to go about life, eh? She went out there saying, "What are the possibilities? What can I create? What can I produce?"

'Others will say "Life's not fair, I'm being stumped, I don't deserve this" — and it was that different mindset that made her an absolute champion. Without doubt it's the foundation of her success.'

Despite her mental prowess and maturity, Lydia does suffer from nerves and stress like the rest of the world's golfers, but she is better able to handle her physiological reaction to stress. In fact, nerves for many golfers are a sign they are in the heat of battle. They welcome the feeling that comes with an adrenaline rush, the shaking hands, the quick breathing, but they also learn to control how this excitement impacts on their ability to wield a club. The best players are not emotionless; they are the best at controlling those emotions.

Managing her physical state — calming the jangling nerves, stilling the racing heart — is what Niethe calls the 'physiology of excellence' which happens in the 'performance window': the time and space in which the golfer is playing a shot.

'One of the first things I taught her was just her simple breathing exercise. As she was progressing in the game, the crowds were getting bigger and she became more aware of the crowds and it was about managing her physiology as she got a little bit nervous . . .'

Lydia has used other little tricks to help her stay in the right mental space, such as writing messages to herself. 'I like to write some quotes or something on my yardage book so that I can refer to it when I get nervous, like "hey, I deserve to be here", or "stay calm", or "do breathing exercises",' she has said. 'Those things kind of help me because when I'm out on the course it's only [caddy] Jason and I that's out there, and I can't go, "Hey, David, can you make me a little less nervous?" or "Can I get a massage?" or whatever. It's just us.'

That said, Niethe believes Lydia is one of those rare people with an inbuilt desire to be on the stage in front of a crowd. His job entailed 'conditioning her to the pressure'.

'There are certain individuals who perform better under pressure. For want of a better analogy I call it the peacock. It's the "look at me, I'm here" personality — Tiger Woods had it and Lydia has it. She loves it, and there's nothing wrong with that. She's a most gracious woman but she draws energy from the crowd and there's something wonderful about being affirmed and acknowledged by millions.'

Another key to Lydia's success is the mental fortress she can build around herself when she enters the 'performance window'.

There are all sorts of 'performance windows' of varying durations in sport — and life. In golf, in a typical round, it's roughly 70 brief windows in which shots are executed.

Within the window, Niethe wanted Lydia to be even-keeled, not too passive, not too aggressive. Assertive. Which means seeing the shot she wants to hit and then committing to it without fear of failure or erring towards the conservative, but also without biting off more than she can achieve.

It also means closing off to all the factors that feed into a shot, whether it's blocking out the pressure of expectation in a big tournament, or shutting out the consequences of a shot. Lydia needs to go into her bubble and close out everything around her that relates to results and focus on the process, says

Otago University sports psychologist Ken Hodge.

'The media, the sponsors, sometimes the coaches, your opponents, even your friends; with them everything is about the winners and the score and all the messages you're getting are about the outcome — we're all obsessed with who wins — so it takes enormous discipline to put that aside and focus on the process.'

Just as important as how she is inside the performance window is how she behaves outside of it. Much of golf is about managing mind and body in all the larger windows between shots. Unlike a fast-paced game of football or a running race, golf offers players huge amounts of downtime between shots. It's a mental desert where a player can easily get lost without the right mind compass.

As Ken Hodge points out, during a four-hour round of golf, the time spent swinging a club is only a matter of minutes; all the rest is downtime.

'I've worked with golfers about their pre-shot routine and process but I've found a lot of success in working on a between-shot routine. What do you do with all that time waiting to play? How do you manage your thoughts? If you can't control your thinking, you can dig yourself into an enormous hole.

'Of course, that is easy to say, much harder to do. I've got great admiration for what this young woman's done.'

One of the other tricks Lydia uses involves her caddy Jason Hamilton.

In her early professional career, she spent a lot of time road-testing different caddies looking for the right person. For her, a caddy was more than a bag carrier or someone who worked out yardages and gave advice on shots; she wanted someone who could take her mind off things in between shots.

In that regard, she was looking for a person who broke one

of the golden rules of caddying — 'show up, keep up, shut up'. She wanted a caddy who chatted.

'My caddy, I like to get him involved. I ask him for his opinion on reading [greens]. He gets my yardages, helps me with club selection, he lines me up . . . so there's not a lot he doesn't do.

'Personality-wise, obviously you can get mad when you make a silly mistake,' she added, saying she wanted a caddy who could make her laugh or take her mind off things.

'I like how Jason makes dumb jokes,' Lydia said. 'He thinks he's doing good jokes but they're pretty bad and he says I'm a Kiwi and he's an Aussie so I don't understand his jokes. I'm pretty sure it's just bad.

'His humour level is not a comedian but sometimes those bad jokes get me over some disappointment because I'm wondering, "What did he say?" I think bad jokes is my criteria.'

Lydia, like all players, will sometimes find herself in a bad patch of form when her swing is off rhythm, or her judgement is not precise. In those situations, she uses techniques to change her body language and outlook. It's the equivalent to smiling when you're feeling down, using the body to send messages to the mind — and not the other way around.

When things aren't going well a player can let their head bow, shoulders sag and gait shuffle, creating a message that they are beaten.

Instead, in those situations, Lydia aims for a state of 'acting as if . . .', using positive body language and a smile — physical cues to try to spark her mind into a more confident state.

Lydia herself has acknowledged this technique, confessing that her external appearance is often at odds with her internal turmoil. 'People say I look like I'm walking on air, that I'm having fun all the time, I'm smiling. Things are really different inside in the head. Sometimes it is hard to play, especially with the expectations and stuff.'

Niethe has also used hypnosis on Lydia, mainly to cement lessons. 'Hypnosis is not a major part of what I use. It ties together all the things I do; out of ten sessions it's probably two.'

The bottom line, however, is that Lydia perfected these difficult techniques because 'she truly was a wonderful student' who came to Niethe with many of the requirements already in place to be a champion, including a huge amount of desire.

'Lots of people ask me: "What's the key to Lydia Ko's success?" And I say to them: "Funny you should use the word key because it represents what makes her a champion." She had a key for the driving range at the Institute of Golf and she needed it because she was often the one who had to lock up.

'There's a saying: "What's done in the dark will shine in the light" and she's a prime example of a girl who was committed to her training — even at night when everyone else was in their bed she was doing her homework after practising her golf . . . she was very self-driven and disciplined.

'I've worked for twenty years in this industry and I still struggle to define what makes a champion. If anything they have a tenacious resolve, they are absolutely determined to make it happen. Lydia had that unshakeable belief in her ability — Lydia believed wholeheartedly right from a very early age.'

The question to Niethe is whether this is learned behaviour or whether some people are born with a different way of thinking to the rest of us.

'They are born with it, but environment tends to enhance it.'

Coach Guy Wilson, for one, believed Lydia possessed an innate ability to detach from pressure. 'You can't train a kid not to feel nervous or threatened, stepping up onto a tee in the New Zealand Open playing professionals,' he said.

Was Lydia born to play golf? She seems to have innately in her possession all the attributes needed — so did she choose golf? Or did golf choose her?

'Call it the law of attraction, the universe, god, whatever,' says Niethe. 'This is a case where the individual chooses the perfect sport for them and then is presented with the perfect support team to help them develop the pathway — that's where the superstars are born from; they just make perfect choices at the perfect time, give or take, and this is what's been created.

'And that came from the time she was handed a club by her aunt and there was a knowing and a connection. It's kind of special, it really is.'

It's the same with gaining her junior membership at Pupuke at seven rather than ten and accelerating her greatness. 'She created that,' Niethe says. 'She demonstrated a commitment to a pursuit of excellence in a chosen sport at a young age when other young kids are maybe dabbling in multiple sports and finding their path in life or not committing to anything.'

And when in that environment earlier than others Lydia showed the same desire to press on.

'Where others are on the golf course, working on the game, she was playing tournaments and developing her game in that cut-throat environment, and she was quite comfortable with that,' Niethe says. 'But she was also able to change her perception of the challenge of it being a golf tournament — it was really just a day on the golf course and that's continued through her career.

'I was talking to her ahead of her first major and I reminded her: "Lyds, a tournament is a tournament, is a tournament — what's different? Has it got fairways? Has it got bunkers? Has it got greens?" It's all perception — and she knew that but it was just reassurance.'

And David Niethe thinks she will keep on creating her own reality, which will typically be different to any other player in history.

'She's very aware of history and is quite motivated by the thought of being the Tiger Woods in the female sense. I think Lydia's capable of being the first female billionaire in sport. She's young, articulate, attractive, charismatic, she has an energy — she's the epitome of excellence: who wouldn't want her to represent their brand?'

'To be a billionaire, that's what she's capable of creating. And she wouldn't do it because of the money — she would want to do it because it hasn't been done before.'

Chapter Fourteen
Million Dollar Baby

Million Dollar Baby. Talk about an easy headline to write for Lydia Ko after she completed her rookie year on the LPGA Tour by winning the biggest prize ever offered in women's golf — a million dollars, stashed inside in a Perspex box.

Her triumph in the 2014 LPGA season-ending championship, renamed the CME Group Tour Championship, and with it the massive bonus payment, took her earnings past $2 million in her first season as a professional.

Her year began in less than auspicious circumstances when she narrowly failed to defend her New Zealand Open title at

Clearwater in Christchurch, losing by a shot to South Korea's Mi Hyang Lee, who shot a blistering final round of nine-under-par 63 to sneak past the home favourite.

It later emerged Lydia had been violently ill before her second round — so sick, in fact, her team suggested she pull out. She refused, saying there were too many people who'd paid good money to come to see her play. New Zealand Golf, in its summary of the event, acknowledged 'bravery and resilience that belied her age. She refused to give up . . . Any way you look at it Lyds is a class act.'

A truer sign of Lydia's class is to look at the transcripts of her press conferences throughout her rookie year on the LPGA. On a circuit such as the LPGA, the players find themselves in a new city each week, facing a bunch of local reporters who ask the same questions as their counterparts from the week before. As a drawcard wherever she goes, Lydia is hauled into the media tent before each event to face a *Groundhog Day* type of experience — the same questions over and over and over again. Mundane is an understatement, yet she answered each time as if it was her first, giving the journalists the headline or soundbite they were looking for.

Between the ho and hum, however, the right question would elicit something more than a stock answer and Lydia would reveal her quirky sense of humour and occasionally offer a slight parting of the iron curtain to reveal an intriguing outlook on life and money.

Asked once if she realised she was a superstar, Lydia turned philosophical: 'I know lots of people call me a superstar and all that. I'm just Lydia. I just want to be me . . . just call me Lydia, you know. It's so comfortable just being you — that's why I love being home, because my friends, they treat me like any other friend and like a teenager and not, "Oh my God, it's her," or oh my God, like taking photos. That's why you've got your friends . . . You can just be known.'

The other constant question — apart from the focus on her ever-present mum — was the Korea–Kiwi connection. Lydia was constantly asked where her allegiances lay or what each country had brought to the mix in the creation of Lydia Ko.

'At home we live like a normal Korean family. We eat Korean food and stuff like that and I like to watch Korean TV,' Lydia explained. 'But I feel the way I act is very Kiwi. I do feel like I have a Kiwi personality. I'm quite freestyle, rather than Korean-style.

'I'm proud to have the [New Zealand] flag on my bag and I had the [silver] fern for a while. I started golf in Korea but did most of my development in New Zealand . . . Obviously when someone looks at me they see a Korean face. I'm proud to be born in Korea and to represent New Zealand and that's something I'm fortunate to have: support from two amazing countries. I'm a Korean Kiwi, or as we say it, Kowi.'

Korean media, while revelling in what Lydia has achieved, refer to her as a New Zealander. And more often than not they use her English name, Lydia, written in Korean script rather than her Korean name, Bogyung. The image she has is more of a New Zealander than a Korean.

New Zealanders, naturally, see her as one of their own — she is after all a New Zealand citizen and flies the Kiwi flag.

Ironically, her mum, Tina, states the nationality issue is not something they think about unless the media raise it. 'We never think about whether we are Korean or Kiwi. It's funny, the only time Lydia has had to think about it is when people started asking her. Lydia lives in New Zealand and she has a New Zealand passport. Lydia plays golf for New Zealand.'

But it was on the subject of money she fielded most questions.

Basically, what does a teenage millionaire spend her money on?

With disarming honesty, Lydia admitted she never saw, nor thought about, any of her prizemoney.

The cheques, she said, went straight into her mother's account and Tina paid out pocket money to her millionaire daughter, with Lydia claiming it was more of a normal existence for her to get money from her mother instead of constantly checking her seven-digit bank balance and imagining what she could buy. And if she ever did spend up large, it was a few hundred dollars, tops.

'I don't really think about money when I'm out here. When they give you the cheque I go, oh, it's $210,000. That's big money, but when I'm out there I'm thinking about making birdies and hitting good shots and making putts rather than, "OK, this putt is going to give me an extra thousand."'

Late April 2014 was one of the more amazing weeks in the already remarkable life of Lydia Ko.

It started with Lydia being named in *Time* magazine's list of 100 most influential people in the world. Six months after the magazine named her one of the most influential teens, she was now alongside some of the most famous faces in the world, including US president Barack Obama.

The list came out the day before she turned 17, with a commentary by Annika Sörenstam, the Swede widely regarded as the best female golfer of the past 30 years.

'Lydia Ko is exceptionally talented, mature beyond her years and well-liked by golf fans and competitors alike,' Sörenstam wrote. 'She is responsible for sparking increased interest in our sport not just in her native South Korea and adopted homeland of New Zealand but also among juniors across the globe.

The cheques went straight into her mother's account and Tina paid out pocket money to her millionaire daughter . . . if she ever did spend up large, it was a few hundred dollars, tops.

'Her early, record-breaking success brings with it incredible pressure — and she's doing a fantastic job handling the many responsibilities that accompany stardom. Her future is very bright. All I can add is to enjoy the ride!'

For her part, Ko lapped up the honour in her inimitable, laidback style.

'Secretly I thought they got it wrong — they got the wrong people. When is my name going to be next to President Obama? Never.

'To be named in that top hundred of the most influential people in the world is huge. Top one hundred in the country is big, but in the whole world, you know, it's a huge honour, especially amongst the big names there.

'I've only been doing what I love to do: playing some fun golf out here on the tour.

'I would love to meet [the other] ninety-nine of those people. All of them. They're big names, apart from me, I think. I would probably go out there with a sketchbook and ask for an autograph from all of them.'

Her seventeenth birthday was also a big occasion as, according to Lydia, it meant she would no longer have people saying to her: 'You're sixteen. You're sixteen. At sixteen you're doing this . . .' She thought: 'It's good to be, I guess, different, seventeen.'

And the week ended with Lydia claiming the Swinging Skirts LPGA Classic in San Francisco with a birdie on the 18th hole to win by a single stroke.

She came to the par-five 18th hole holding a slender one-shot lead over playing partners Stacy Lewis and Jenny Shin. It looked like she'd blown her chance when she hit her second shot into heavy rough, making for a tough approach to an elevated green where Lewis and Shin had already given themselves birdie opportunities which could have forced a play-off.

If either player sensed the door ajar, Lydia slammed it shut with a nerveless pitch and dead-eye putt to score her first win as a paid-up member of the LPGA tour.

To make the win even more special was the fact that — for the first time — Gil Hong was on hand to see her win an LPGA event.

Lydia only just held back tears after her winning putt and again at the victory ceremony. 'You may lose friends, but you're never going to lose your parents. They're always with you. I think that's why it actually made me feel a little bit more emotional. I try and make myself not cry of happiness, but it was coming to that point.'

Stacy Lewis, who had seen a lot of Lydia already in her short career, was again full of admiration for her young rival. 'I expected her to do exactly what she did today. Her best quality is that whenever she needs to make a shot or needs to make a putt she does. It's pretty hard to beat someone when they do that.'

The win meant a huge deal to Lydia, so much so, she later went out and commemorated it by getting her first tattoo. Inscribed on the inside of her left wrist is: IV-XXVII-XIV, a Roman letters rendition of the American-style date of her victory, 4-27-14 (April 27, 2014).

Within a couple of months, any doubt about Lydia's decision to fast-forward her professional career was obliterated with her win at the Marathon Classic in Toledo, Ohio. The prizemoney from that event in July tipped her earnings past US$1 million, making her the youngest millionaire in LPGA history.

The win came in stunning fashion, with Lydia setting her sights on posting a final round of six-under-par 65, a score she figured would give her a chance of victory.

Her sixth birdie of the day — to match her forecast — came on the par-five 18th, and when Korean So Yeon Ryu missed her birdie putt, Lydia had scored a one-shot win and her second title of the year.

The win took her to the Women's PGA Championship at Monroe Golf Club in Pittsford, New York with expectations she could become the first 17-year-old to win a women's major title.

A final-round charge, with three birdies in four holes, put her right on the heels of the two leaders, Inbee Park and American Brittany Lincicome, but the normally steely Kiwi faltered in the home stretch with a bogey-bogey finish, dropping her into a tie for third place and three shots out of a play-off, where Inbee Park triumphed.

Lydia came to the final event of the year with a chance to claim the $1 million bonus prize for finishing at the top of the season-long points race known as Race to CME Globe, introduced by the LPGA in 2014.

She'd also claimed the Rookie of the Year title, which meant she had to give a speech at the season-ending dinner on the Friday night halfway through the tournament. Of all the things Lydia did in 2014, her acceptance speech went the furthest in winning friends and influencing people, despite her confession to feeling more nerves about public speaking than playing for a million dollars at the weekend.

Turns out she needn't have worried, wrote Steve DiMeglio in *USA Today*: 'Ko killed it,' he wrote. 'In front of a microphone she's at ease . . . even if she doesn't realise it.'

Starting with a joke about needing a shot of vodka to calm her nerves, the too-young-to-legally-drink Lydia had the room in stitches as she thanked all the caddies who helped in her rookie season, ticking off their first names one by one. All 10 of them.

Lydia consulted friend and rival Stacy Lewis about what she was going to say, telling Stacy she was going to make fun of herself. 'I said go ahead. She doesn't take herself too seriously. She's just a great person to be around.'

That self-effacing nature and easy Kiwi charm won plenty of admiration from her peers — but on the weekend, the laughs stopped and the killer instinct kicked in as she claimed the season-ending championship in a three-way play-off over Carlota Ciganda of Spain and Julieta Granada of Paraguay. The play-off lasted four holes, with Lydia's unrelenting accuracy and ability to play error-free golf creating victory as each of her rivals stumbled.

They played the 18th hole four times, with Lydia playing the hole in identical fashion each time, driving the ball to the same spot in the fairway, having the same yardage to the hole — and executing perfectly each time as one by one her rivals faltered.

It was vintage Ko, if such a term can be used for a rookie; she eliminated mistakes and played like a machine.

As she received her Perspex box full of cash, commentator Judy Rankin described her as the 'Million Dollar Baby'.

'That's not a bad nickname,' Lydia said later, before playing down the size of the winning bonus when asked how her friends might regard her millionaire status.

'It is huge money, you know. Even a thousand dollars is huge money. For us, a hundred dollars is huge money. But the great thing about my friends is most of them don't play golf. When I'm hanging around with them, we don't talk about golf or the hook I hit on seven or whatever. So that's what I really love. I kind of feel like I can get off the course, get my mind free, and just be that teenager.'

As ESPN noted in a report on her incredible rookie season, to Lydia, money was an abstract notion. She didn't seem to need it — with her mother and family taking care of everything she needs — and she certainly doesn't flaunt it: 'She even dresses in a way that doesn't elicit attention,' wrote the *New York Times* after her victory in the Tour Championship, 'favouring primary colours while her fellow competitors explore the cerises and electric limes in the Crayola box. She wore solid blue pants on Sunday, but pushed her comfort zone by wearing a blue-and-white striped shirt.'

Chapter Fifteen

Sharper focus

A symbol of transition, a marketing ploy or just something to help her play better? Those were among the opinions being cast when the LPGA media guide for the 2015 season appeared featuring a glasses-free, un-ponytailed Lydia Ko.

Lydia's makeover gave the New Zealand media plenty to feast on as they ticked off the long summer days ahead of the Cricket World Cup.

Lydia's dark-rimmed glasses had become a trademark throughout her amateur career but they were something she'd longed to ditch — if possible.

In Thailand a year earlier, she'd shared a press conference with Stacy Lewis and the question came up about laser eye surgery, which a number of golfers had undergone — notably

Tiger Woods.

'I want to get rid of these,' Lydia said, pointing to her glasses.

Stacy warned she had to wait until she was a little older to even consider eye surgery. 'She's not old enough yet. That's the problem,' she said of the then 16-year-old.

Without glasses, Lydia reckoned she'd only be able to see shadows and blurred outlines — and that she definitely wouldn't be able to recognise people.

'If I didn't wear my glasses I would not be able to hit the ball straight. So, you know, I'm lucky that there is stuff like glasses for people to actually be able to see and things like contacts,' she said, with typically Ko-like wonderment. 'So I think that's one of the amazing things that has been created in this world.'

It turns out, though, the glasses were a hassle on course, slipping down her nose when she sweated, getting wet when it rained. So in 2015 she changed to contact lenses, with the hope one day she would undergo laser eye surgery.

'The glasses had become my "Lydia Ko look",' she admitted, saying she struggled to recognise herself when she looked in the mirror for the first time after she switched to contact lenses.

'Initially it felt like everything was bigger — I looked at my hands and thought, "They didn't seem this big."'

Suffering the 'awkward' feeling of going out on the golf course without something perched on her nose, she wore lensless glasses to help her adjust in her season-opening round before ditching them for the second round.

Of course, an array of commentators had opinions on the matter, especially about the glam shot in the LPGA media guide which projected a more mature look. 'If Ko is trying to make a statement — I'm not a kid anymore and I mean business — it's working!' wrote golf.com.

Lydia herself noted 2015 was all about change, including

new caddy Jason Hamilton to go with her relatively new coach: 'Different caddy, different coach, different look, I'm older, a lot of things [are] different. The only thing is I have the same name. Yeah, that's the only thing that is the same. But change is — sometimes there is a saying if it's good, why do you fix it? But we fix it sometimes to try to get better.'

The first statement in a giant exclamation mark of a year came, ironically, at the end of January when she blew the lead in the Coates Championship in Florida, surrendering a four-shot lead to Na Yeon Choi to finish in a tie for second place. But the result — and the associated ranking points — propelled her to No. 1 in the Women's World Golf Rankings.

And not just any world No. 1 — the youngest ever (male or female) to top the global rankings, taking over from Tiger Woods, who was crowned the men's No. 1 when he was 21 years, 167 days. Still months away from her 18th birthday, Lydia was just 17 years, 283 days when she ascended to the top of the world.

Another emphatic statement came the following month at the Australian Women's Open, played at the famed Royal Melbourne golf course on what's known as the Melbourne sandbelt — a string of courses famed around the world for their unique beauty and demanding layouts.

In many ways the tournament harked back to her childhood years, many of which were spent decoding the puzzle of Titirangi, the course she first attacked as a seven-year-old in the New Zealand Women's Stroke Play Championship and the site of her epic battle with Cecilia Cho as a 12-year-old.

What Titirangi and Royal Melbourne have in common is a design by Alister MacKenzie, who loved to examine a golfer's understanding of the way the game should be played. His courses put primacy on position rather than length, and reward smart play over brute strength, which has become the hallmark of Lydia's game.

Royal Melbourne, like Titirangi, is all about angles and playing from the right part of the fairway. But because it is in the sandbelt region, the course can become baked dry and the greens, in particular, bone-hard.

Under those conditions it becomes treacherous even for the best players in the world. So much so that Stacy Lewis said she wouldn't play the Australian Open because the course didn't reward good shots.

To the contrary, no course better rewards good shots; it's just that Stacy failed to understand the right shots. What she meant was, it didn't reward the usual high irons into greens favoured by American players. Instead of the balls sticking to the green they would simply roll off the back.

Lydia, at just 17, had solved the code. She was the only player to have all four rounds under par and won by two shots. During the tournament she hit an incredible 64 of 72 greens in regulation.

Mike Clayton, the Australian golf course architect and former touring pro, followed Lydia around for her final round and came away singing her praises, comparing her to one of the greats of the men's game, Spain's golfing magician Seve Ballesteros.

'She dismantled that course really,' he said on the State of the Game podcast. 'I watched Seve there in 1978 and whilst it was much different it was just as impressive. It was almost the most impressive golf I've seen at Royal Melbourne. She just took it apart, she understood it, hit it in the perfect spots and put it on the greens . . .'

This under conditions bordering unfair, with the greens running faster than any on the PGA Tour. 'It got to be like a

Plenty hit it further and higher. But when it comes to getting the ball in the hole, there are few better players.

skating rink at the end, but of course Lydia belied that by playing the course perfectly and showing it was perfectly playable.'

Like the American wunderkind Jordan Spieth, about to announce himself to the world as the Masters champion at another MacKenzie course, Augusta, Lydia doesn't wow casual observers with her game, Clayton said. Plenty hit it further and higher. But when it comes to getting the ball in the hole, there are few better players. It's their course management that sets them apart, a skill illuminated by courses such as Royal Melbourne and Titirangi (and Augusta for the men).

'Royal Melbourne more than anywhere rewards good shots, it just murders shots that are average or played from the wrong side or land in the wrong spot,' Clayton said. 'Pros, their idea of a good shot is a shot out of the middle that goes in a nice trajectory, goes where it's aimed and hits the green and stops.'

Lydia had understood, he said, that Royal Melbourne 'asks different questions' of a golfer, to which the answer is the art of hitting a variety of golf shots, such as the 'shot that's got to land forty feet short and left of the hole with a low fade and bounce and run up through the swale and leak its way to a back right pin . . .'

According to Clayton, Lydia had shown that understanding at Royal Melbourne.

'On the 15th hole, every day, she just hit a perfect shot to that green, landed it in the same spot, exactly the right spot with the right trajectory and bounced the ball back to the hole. She actually hit it in the hole one day.'

Given Spieth's success at Augusta, with one green jacket and two runner-up finishes, it's just a pity the women don't get to play there because it's a course designed to suit Lydia's game to a tee. Creative short game: check. Precise with irons: check.

Good putter: check. And of course, most importantly, good temperament.

Maybe — as the men's and women's tours come into closer alignment — the masters of Augusta will one day host a women's major and we will get to watch what Lydia can do on what is the best-known MacKenzie-designed course.

From Melbourne, where, by the way — and as can be expected — she was the youngest winner in Australian Open history, Lydia showed how much debt she owed New Zealand Golf by contesting the New Zealand Women's Open at Clearwater in Christchurch at the end of February.

The relatively paltry prizemoney, the interference it played with her schedule, the pressure from sponsors and management to play in bigger events in Asia — all were cast aside as she returned home to win her second national title by a comfortable margin. Indicative of her importance for golf in New Zealand was the presence of Prime Minister John Key walking the course along with other fans.

Not yet 18 years old, with 10 worldwide titles to her name, many millions in the bank — despite all she had achieved, Lydia came to the first major of the year, the ANA Inspiration at Mission Hills Country Club, in Rancho Mirage, California, with the acid on her to deliver the one prize golf uses to measure status: a major championship.

And there's no doubt the pressure of major championship golf gnawed at her — especially as all and sundry expected her to add another 'youngest ever . . .' tag to her list by beating Morgan Pressel's mark as the youngest woman to win a major at 18 years, 313 days.

'The majors, they give me butterflies a lot. I really shouldn't think of it as a different tournament or different scale, but somehow I just go there and I don't feel like my game is up to the standard,' Lydia reflected. 'I'm trying to learn to . . . to handle myself, calm myself, and take myself back a little bit and say, "You know what? This is just another tournament."'

Acutely aware of Morgan Pressel's piece of history — carved out at the same Mission Hills venue in 2007 — Lydia jokingly said the pressure of winning a major at a younger age than Morgan would only disappear once she turned 19.

'Obviously [because of] Morgan's record, there's a lot of talk about this major-winning deal, because there is that record. But to me, I would just love to win *a* major sometime from now and twelve years [when she plans to retire], just sometime then.'

Her other driver for a major win was the fact her sponsor, Callaway, gives all its men's and women's major winners a golden putter as a reward. Like meeting movie stars or getting her ears pierced in her younger days, the golden putter was her incentive.

Lydia came to the ANA Inspiration with another record in her sights . . . up until that point she had played 28 consecutive rounds under par. Only Annika Sörenstam, with 29 rounds in a row under par, had done better. The expectation, when Lydia opened with a one-under-par 71 and tied Sörenstam's mark at 29, was that she would break the record in the second round.

She came to the final hole, the difficult par-five 18th, needing a birdie to record another 71 and a 30th round on the trot under par . . . but ended up with a bogey six, a round of 73 and level with one of her childhood idols in a meaningless but nevertheless compelling statistic which is a measure of consistency.

Lydia, of course, made light of it, saying when she stuffs up a hole she normally improves on the next hole. But in this case 'there's no 19th hole. That's apparently the bar . . . I'm not hitting the bar.'

Lydia finished in a tie for 51st — and as the clock ticked down on her chances to surpass Morgan as the youngest major winner, she returned to the scene of her inaugural LPGA triumph, at the Swinging Skirts tournament in San Francisco.

Mid-tournament cake and candles for her 18th birthday and a dinner at a Korean barbecue restaurant didn't distract her in a week of double celebrations as she chased down — of all people — Morgan Pressel in the final round to force a play-off, which she won on the second hole of sudden death.

The meaning of the moment — one teen prodigy beating a former teen prodigy who hadn't won an LPGA tournament for seven years — wasn't lost on the scribes.

It opened the door for questions on Morgan's record and Lydia's missing major, with Lydia admitting she had tried to force things too hard at the ANA Inspiration because she knew how little time she had to deliver.

'Sometimes I try and force it a little bit. Weeks like ANA, I kind of tried so hard and tried to force some good scores and I tried to force everything, and that's when I didn't play as good. So I think one of the big things is really self-pressure. I've been talking to David Niethe, talking to David [Leadbetter] and Sean [Hogan] and trying to just enjoy the moment, and that's all I can do. I can't think about the past and I can't think about what's coming.'

What was coming? In June, something completely unexpected . . . at the next major championship, the Women's PGA at Westchester Country Club in New York, Lydia missed the cut for the first time in her life. After 53 consecutive tournaments where she'd played every round, she finally had a week to forget, her first week without a pay cheque, and for the first time in her life she went home early from an event.

The missed cut also meant Lydia surrendered her No. 1 world ranking, as Inbee Park reclaimed the top spot based on the rolling points system used in the rankings.

This rare Lydia blip immediately prompted questions from the sidelines: was she burnt out? Had David Leadbetter's weird swing plan ruined her? Had the pressure got to her? Now, at 18, had the carefree approach of her earlier years disappeared? Was the pressure of the missing major too much for her?

As if . . . Lydia answered her critics with a string of good results, a sixth place in Arkansas, a tie for 12th with a solid performance at the US Open, and she finished just one shot out of a play-off as she tried to defend her title at the Marathon Classic.

She later said her mid-season slump owed a lot to momentarily losing her life-long bearings, forgetting to have fun. 'I kind of lost having fun a little bit and found out how important it was to me to have fun and have a smile on my face.'

She went into the Women's British Open in August in good form at the famed — but now infamous — Turnberry course in Scotland. Famed because of its history, including the historic 'Duel in the Sun' between Jack Nicklaus and Tom Watson at the Open Championship in 1977; infamous because the course had just been purchased by Donald Trump and renamed Trump Turnberry. Trump's views on Mexicans, Muslims and Chinese were considered so toxic, the sport's governing body in Britain, the R&A, removed Turnberry from the list of courses on the Open Championship rota in December 2015.

Trump even managed to steal the headlines during the first round when his massive helicopter circled the course twice before landing, the property magnate jumping out to survey his kingdom.

The noisy arrival briefly distracted Lydia on the 16th hole as she blazed through the first round in 66 to lie one behind former amateur rival Hyo Joo Kim of South Korea.

Afterwards as media huffed and puffed about the egotistical Trump's ability to upstage the event, *Herald Scotland* writer Nick Rodger suggested taking a leaf out of Lydia's book.

'Perhaps we all need to adopt the shrugging nonchalance of the happy-go-lucky teenager, Lydia Ko,' he wrote, referring to her reaction when Trump circled overhead in his chopper.

'"I was on the 16th and I saw the helicopter and I was like man, that's a really nice helicopter, I'd love one", she said after launching her bid for a maiden major title with a six-under 66 to sit just a shot off the lead.'

In sideways rain and freezing conditions on the second day, her battling 73 kept her in the hunt behind leader Suzann Pettersen.

The weekend had a quirky twist when another Ko, 20-year-old Korean Jin-Young Ko, jumped to the top of the leaderboard, with Lydia close behind, three shots adrift. 'People think we're related,' Jin-Young said, before clarifying they were not.

Before the tournament Lydia had told media her biggest worry on the golf course was its famed pot bunkers, deep, with vertical walls. 'I think the really big thing is not to hit it in the pot bunkers. David [Leadbetter] said because I'm not that tall, every bunker is a pot bunker to me.'

As it turned out, the pot bunker on the 12th hole in the final round proved Lydia's downfall, as her second shot came to rest against one of the steep faces. Her attempt to get the ball out saw it hit the wall in front of her and then scuttle around the curved face until it ended up behind her. All she could do — in typical fashion — was laugh.

Forced to hit out backwards for her fourth shot, she carded

a double bogey and another major title hope was buried. She ended up third behind Inbee Park, who was fast becoming to the professional Lydia what Cecilia Cho had been as an amateur — someone for her to chase down.

At this stage, Inbee was so far ahead she may as well have been on a different course — the British Open was her seventh major championship and it cemented her status as the world No. 1.

Like Cecilia, Inbee was as much a friend as a rival to Lydia.

'They both push each other,' said Brad Beecher, Inbee's Australian caddy. 'No matter what week it is, one of them is playing outstanding golf. It inspires the other one to play better. I don't know that it's a rivalry where they feel like "I must beat her". I think it's more like "I want to be as good as her. I want to do what she's doing".'

Lydia's caddy, Jason Hamilton, thought the two players brought out the best in each other.

'Inbee's a great player,' Hamilton said. 'She drags you up. She has that effect on people.'

It was another friendly rival who stood in Lydia's way as she set about claiming a third Canadian Open title in four years — Stacy Lewis.

Stacy had been on hand when Lydia won her first Canadian Open as an amateur, guiding the then 15-year-old through the jangling nerves as she walked down the 18th fairway with the 2012 title in the bag.

In the interim Stacy had become something of a mentor to Lydia. As one of the leading players in the world, the American was often paired with the rising star during her early professional career as organisers sought to create marquee groups for the fans and TV broadcasters.

At the 2015 Canadian Open they were head to head again, this time in a play-off for the title, which Lydia quickly decided with a tap-in par putt on the first hole to leave Stacy deflated. But if she was worried about ever beating the Kiwi kid, she didn't show it.

The pair bumped fists as they stood on the first play-off hole, which Stacy said was an acknowledgement of how well they'd come to know each other since that first Canadian Open together in 2012.

'We've just played so much golf together. We are just both comfortable out there playing together and both comfortable being in a play-off. We're just good friends and she's easy to play with. I played with her here when she was fifteen when she won. Just a good person to play with.'

And, of course, the win sent Lydia to the season's final major — in France — with a heavy burden: it would be her last chance to oust Morgan Pressel from the record books as the youngest major winner in women's golf.

Chapter Sixteen
Number crunching

Golf is a game of numbers and one of the most talked-about numbers in golf is 63.

It's the lowest score ever shot in a men's major championship. In the thousands upon thousands of rounds of golf played at major championships two dozen men have shot 63 but no one — not Tiger Woods, Greg Norman or Jack Nicklaus — has gone lower than 63.

But for many years one 63 stood out. Until Sweden's Henrik Stenson joined him in 2016, Johnny Miller was the only player to shoot 63 in the final round of a major *and* win the tournament, which he did in claiming the US Open in 1973 at the demanding Oakmont layout. Stenson matched that when he carded 63 in the final round at Royal Troon to claim his first major — the Open Championship — in July 2016.

So for golf journalists — who thrive on these things — a 63 in the final round of a major championship is a benchmark for audacity and brilliance.

In the women's game, there have been lower scores in major championships: Hyo Joo Kim holds the record with a 61 shot en route to winning the Evian Championship in 2014.

And when the field lined up in September for the 2015 Evian Championship on the shores of Lake Geneva in France, there had been a couple of 62s in majors and three 63s — but no one had shot 63 (or better) in the final round of a women's major. And certainly no woman had been able to match Miller's feat of shooting a closing round 63 to claim the title.

There are reasons low scores are hard to come by in the final round of a major. First, the courses are invariably set up much harder than a normal tournament and, second, the final round is usually set up harder still. The last day is generally when the greens are at their firmest and fastest, when the rough is longest and when the pin placements are the most inaccessible. The last day of a major championship is usually about hanging tough, not blazing away for a low score.

Lydia Ko entered the final day of the Evian Championship in touch with the leaders. At eight under par she was tied for third alongside Morgan Pressel, two shots adrift of leader Mi Hyang Lee and one behind Lexi Thompson.

By the seventh hole — after Mi Hyang had dropped away with an early double-bogey — it had become a two-woman race between Lydia and Lexi, who made four birdies in her opening seven holes to lead Lydia by three.

A bogey to Lexi followed by a birdie to Lydia reduced the deficit to just one shot. Back-to-back birdies on 11 and 12 lifted the teen Kiwi to the lead by one with five holes to play, as a neck-and-neck finish beckoned.

Major championships, as Lydia found at the British Open with her pot-bunker experience, can be won or lost on one hole . . . but she wasn't going to make any mistakes this time. Instead, on the par-three 14th it was Lexi who lost control of her tee shot and sent her ball sailing into deep rough. She needed two chunky chips to escape the long grass and two putts later she had a double-bogey five on her card and trailed Lydia by three with four holes to play.

Not one to let a rival off the hook with a big catch so close, Lydia birdied three of the last four holes, shot a nine-under-par 63 and won by six.

At 18 years and 142 days old, Lydia Ko took the crown as the youngest major champion in women's history. And for the first time on the course as a professional, Lydia showed some real emotion as the tears welled up after the last putt had fallen.

As commentator Paige Mackenzie noted in the aftermath, those tears showed how much the win meant.

'When she first started winning, the biggest concern was that she would wake up one day and realise how good she is and it would freak her out — because it looked so effortless, as if she didn't understand the magnitude of the events she was winning. Today we saw her understand — you saw her tearing up on the 18th green, you knew what this event meant to her. She understood the magnitude of what she'd done.'

'Yeah, a couple teardrops,' Lydia confessed. 'I didn't totally cry-cry but I kind of got a little overwhelmed, and I could kind of feel tears coming when Jason said, "Enjoy the moment," coming down onto the green. I kind of felt back over the whole week and all the questions I've been asked.'

'It's kind of hard to beat somebody that shoots sixty-three,' Lexi Thompson said afterwards. 'She played amazing. She deserves it. She ball-struck the heck out of this golf course and putted it really well. You can't get much better than that.'

For Lydia it meant the end of *that* question. 'Everyone won't be asking me when I'll win my first major because it's done,' she said.

To put Lydia's achievement into perspective, she became not only the youngest female major winner but the youngest winner of a major in nearly 150 years. The record, which seems like it will never be beaten, is held by Young Tom Morris — who was 17 years old when he won the 1868 British Open.

Given the state of golf in 1868 — the field comprised fewer than two dozen players, it had nowhere near the media attention it gets now, the money at stake was slim and depth of competition slimmer — Lydia's triumph is now the benchmark for all young golfers, male or female.

There is little reprieve for a modern professional golfer — even those who shoot 63 in the final round to become the youngest ever major championship winner in history — and Lydia had only a few days to celebrate her triumph before she hit the road again for the Asian swing of the LPGA Tour, and setting more records.

First up in October was the Taiwan Championship in Taipei. By winning this by a whopping nine strokes Lydia not only returned to the top of the world rankings ahead of Inbee Park, but she clocked her 10th LPGA title and — you guessed it — became the youngest player to claim 10 titles on either the PGA or LPGA by some margin.

Horton Smith had held the men's record of winning 10 titles when he was 21, while fellow American Nancy Lopez, one of the greats of the women's game, was 22 when she lifted her 10th trophy.

The victory in Taiwan set up another duel with Inbee Park for a raft of honours at the season-ending CME Group Tour Championship, where Lydia had won the $1 million bonus pay-day in 2014.

There was the tournament itself, the Race to CME Globe and its $1 million bonus (decided by a points-based battle created to make the season finale more spectacular), the LPGA Player of the Year battle (another points-based contest but separate to the $1 million pay-day), the Vare Trophy for lowest scoring average on the tour based on average score per round, and — finally — the season-ending world No. 1 ranking, which was at stake as well.

It is as complicated as it sounds, so much so that when Lydia finished the tournament in Florida for a tie for sixth place at 12 under par, an identical score to Inbee Park, she had no idea what it meant. 'I didn't know how these points worked out. I didn't know if sixth place was good enough or whatever. My mind kind of went completely blank, but at the same time was trying to calculate things that I don't know how to calculate.'

The computers spat out the information: Lydia had won the Race to CME Globe and the million-dollar pay-day for the second time, and became just the fourth player in history — and the first since Annika Sörenstam — to go from being Rookie of the Year to Player of the Year the following season.

Again, as at Evian, the tears started to flow.

'I'm so happy that my team was here with me because it wasn't only me that was working hard, it was the whole team. Everybody was working so hard to get better and have that

Lydia became just the fourth player in history to go from being Rookie of the Year to Player of the Year the following season.

more consistent season. For them to be here with me, just a lot of emotions and it's probably the most I'll cry on TV ever.'

Lydia didn't sweep all the awards on offer, however, with Inbee Park claiming the Vare Trophy for the best scoring average and Inbee had done enough — based on another points system — to be inducted into the LPGA Hall of Fame.

And 38-year-old US mother Cristie Kerr won the tournament — a wonderful story in itself to counteract the surge of youth on the tour. Cristie paid tribute to Lydia's amazing achievements in her press conference.

'I don't think she's the age she is. She's such an old soul, it's hard to believe she's that young. She's been winning tournaments since she was thirteen or fourteen out here. What is she, eighteen now? I'm over twice her age. That's crazy.'

Cristie was full of praise for Lydia's even temperament.

'She just has such a great way about her. She doesn't seem to worry about much. I worry about everything, especially being a mom now. I guess maybe that's youth. . . . But she has such a great, easy disposition about her. She puts everybody around her at ease. I think she'll be that way for the rest of her life. I think that's just her personality.'

Old soul or not, Lydia wasn't yet done with the youngest-ever business. But before she achieved another landmark feat she found time to return home to New Zealand in early 2016 to defend her national title, where tears were to flow again.

There are so many ingredients in the pot of Lydia's greatness, from her parents, to Guy Wilson, to the team at the Institute of Golf, the rivalry with Cecilia Cho, her new coaches, her caddy . . . but as a young player coming through amateur ranks she also benefited from knowing one of the greatest women to have been involved in New Zealand golf, Patsy Hankins.

Hankins, a former president of New Zealand Golf and among the first women given membership of the Royal and Ancient Golf Club of St Andrews in Scotland, was a trailblazing administrator renowned for her kind and gentle approach.

Whenever she could, she travelled to major events with New Zealand women's teams and always made sure she was on hand for young players who needed a shoulder to cry on or a word of wisdom.

Emily Perry, an amateur teammate of Lydia's, described Hankins as an inspirational woman, 'fiercely passionate' and with a unique way of inspiring and lifting young players.

'Say if you had a bad round, she'd come out with something that made you feel so much better and so inspired and you'd be thinking, "Where did that come from?" It came from experience and all the events she'd been to and all the golfers she'd seen — and she was so proud to be there for the New Zealand team.

'It made all the difference to have someone who was a friend who you could go and talk to and she'd always pop up with this fierce, unexpected passion. She was so refreshing and different.

'Anyone who played for New Zealand had a special bond with Patsy.'

When Hankins passed away in late 2015, Lydia was playing in Taiwan, and after her nine-shot win she paid tribute to her former mentor, saying news of her death, aged 70, 'broke my heart'.

'I think I was really playing for Patsy this week. She was such a huge factor in my life in my junior golf. To hear that she had passed away was very hard to hear and I'm so happy that I can bring this win to her and her family.'

In coming back to Clearwater Resort for the New Zealand Open in February 2016, the memories of Hankins rose to the surface again ahead of the tournament. Lydia remembered her first Open win at the venue as an amateur in 2013, when Hankins presented her the trophy.

'For me there are so many great memories — the big thing about my first win here was that Patsy Hankins was there . . . I'm getting emotional here . . . and we did the trophy shot together . . . oh man,' she said as tears welled up.

'Patsy was such a special person and for her to be there at my first time winning the national open . . . it's one of the reasons I look forward to coming back.'

Tears flowed again after she claimed the title and, in her acceptance speech, thanked New Zealand Golf for all the support they'd given her over her amateur career.

'There's no bigger word than thank you . . . oh, I'm going to cry,' she said. 'I want to thank you guys for always having hope in me. With my South Korean background there was always doubt: is she going back to Korea? Is she going to stay?

'But you stuck with me and made it easier for me and I wouldn't be here without you guys — you are a huge part of my career. And that's why I miss Patsy even more,' she said, failing this time to hold back the tears.

The poignancy of the moment said so much about the person Lydia Ko had become.

Chapter Seventeen
Golden girl

If you set out on a journey to find someone who would have a bad word to say about Lydia Ko, you'd be walking for a very long time.

High-level sport is a cut-throat business and like anything with money and status at its heart it is full of egos, but Lydia Ko is universally loved by her peers, the media, the public, the sponsors . . .

'I've not heard anyone say a bad word about her, which is pretty extraordinary at this high level of sport. That says it all, really,' says Englishwoman Laura Davies, who has spent four decades in golf.

It's not like Lydia is a saint — at least not in the Mother Teresa mould — but to those used to the rampant egos and self-aggrandisers of modern sport, she's the next closest thing. Or, as her friend Michelle Wie once joked: 'I heard her swear once, so she's not perfect . . . I don't know how a person can be that nice. I would probably explode inside.'

At the start of the 2015 LPGA season, Lydia's second season on tour, she returned to Florida from New Zealand with excess luggage: big boxes of New Zealand-made Whittaker's chocolate. She put a large bar in the locker of all the players gathered at her first event of the season with a note tucked inside which read: 'This is where I made my first start as a rookie last year, and I just wanted to thank everyone for being super nice to me all year.'

The reaction from fellow season professionals was best summed up by Morgan Pressel: 'I don't know that any player's ever put a gift in everybody's locker. That's the thing about Lydia. She seems to do all the right things.'

For Lydia, it was as simple as breathing. It wasn't a forced gesture or something artificial — she didn't get one of her minions to go to a local supermarket and buy whatever was on special, she wanted to give her peers a slice of New Zealand, something that represented her. It was a gesture from the heart.

A couple of weeks later she was back in the southern hemisphere, contesting the Australian Open at Royal Melbourne. After dissecting the course to claim the trophy, she sought out Royal Melbourne's assistant general manager Andrea Watson with an envelope containing $500 and asked for it to be put on the bar to help the volunteers wind down with a few free drinks.

The gesture left Royal Melbourne chief executive Paul Rak gobsmacked. 'I've worked in the golf industry for forty years and I've never heard of anything like that — especially from a seventeen-year-old,' he said.

'Lydia Ko is a class act — I can't say enough about her. She made a good impression on a lot of people, that's for sure . . . and made a lot of our staff and volunteers very happy. She's a credit to golf and those around her.'

Others remember a remarkable night at the end of her 2012 season in New Zealand when the late golf commentator Phillip Leishman hosted a Q&A session with Lydia at the Gulf Harbour club as part of an evening to celebrate an incredible year.

At the end, Leishman asked Lydia if there was anyone she'd like to thank.

'If I'm going to thank people I'd better stand up,' Lydia said.

And with that, according to those in attendance, she went around a crowded room table by table, without notes or preparation, and thanked every single person who had made the smallest contribution to her success.

Lydia is also renowned for the spirit in which she plays the game — her Twitter and Instagram accounts are full of congratulatory messages to her rivals when they do well. While there is a greater sense of camaraderie on the women's tour than on the men's PGA, Lydia's constant support and encouragement of her fellow competitors does raise eyebrows.

The most notable example was when she played in the final group alongside young Korean Ha Na Jang in the Coates Championship in Florida in early 2016. Jang had been oh-so-close to winning her first tournament on numerous occasions but had fallen just short each time and there was a question mark over her ability to get the job done.

In the final round Lydia had fallen off the pace and couldn't win the tournament, but instead of going into her own world and wondering what the heck went wrong, she became Jang's No. 1 cheerleader and support, urging her on as rain set in and the afternoon grew cold and dark.

Jang held on by her fingernails to win from young Canadian Brooke Henderson and afterwards paid tribute to Lydia's encouragement.

'Lydia, she say, "Ha Na, you can do it. You're more confident and comfortable in your mind, no problem. Keep going, keep going."'

It was the same a few weeks later when Lydia was pipped for her second Australian Open title by Japan's Haru Nomura, who played outstandingly under pressure over the closing holes. Lydia was in the group ahead of Nomura and could easily have signed her card, completed her media obligations and wandered off to ponder what might have been. But instead she headed straight back out to the 18th green to join other players who raced up to Nomura once the final putt had gone down and doused her with water, which has become a trademark celebration on the LPGA Tour.

Randall Mell, for Golf Channel, described Lydia as 'chasing Nomura around with two bottles of water in giddy, childlike delight'.

The greatest test of Lydia's attitude to rivals — and defeat — came at the Women's PGA Championship in June 2016 at the Sahalee Country Club in Washington state.

Sahalee, in the language of the Chinookan people, means 'heavenly high ground', and it looked destined to be just that for Lydia as she led for most of a thrilling final round before finding herself in a play-off with Brooke Henderson, who at 18 is just a few months younger than Lydia and seems to have the same mental fortitude as her Kiwi rival. Henderson made the play-off after a spectacular recovery from a tough position behind a forked tree on the 18th hole — drilling her ball through a gap in the trees, she was able to scramble a par and ensure the tournament went to extra holes.

‘I don’t believe in golf gods. Good bounces and bad ones are random. I’m Catholic and believe in God — the big God — and what’s important is to believe that He believes in you. If you don’t believe in God, that’s fine, too. There are many perspectives in the world.’

— Lydia Ko, aged 16

The riveting shot-making continued in the play-off, with Henderson spearing her approach shot right at the flag and leaving herself a simple short putt for her first major championship.

As the camera panned across the green it fell on Lydia, applauding generously as she acknowledged the fact she was outgunned by a youngster as seemingly impervious to pressure as herself.

Applauding Henderson, encouraging Jang, joining in celebrations for her conquerors, sending messages of congratulations — it's impossible to imagine Tiger Woods doing anything remotely similar when he was at the top of the men's game. Lydia's behaviour is atypical of a world No. 1 in any sport, and she certainly doesn't have the arrogance and insularity associated with other world-class performers.

It harks back to her own mental approach to the game, where her philosophy is to do the best she can and if it's good enough, so be it. If she's not good enough, she's certainly not going to resent anyone else who performs well. She badly wants to win, but she doesn't want it at anyone else's expense. Even more than that, according to her coach David Leadbetter, 'she's actually wanting other players to play well'.

Her emotional wellbeing is not tied to beating others but to performing as well as she can, so it helps create a disposition resembling inner peace.

'She has an unbelievable temperament; nothing rattles her,' Leadbetter has said. 'Kelly, my wife, said it looks like she walks on water. There is this aura about her. There is no one quite like Lydia Ko and never has been. The other great players [throughout history] were very, very intense.'

Leadbetter has compared Lydia's outlook with that of his other star pupil Nick Faldo, saying Faldo had two personalities

— his easy-going, fun-loving, off-the-course persona and his on-course self-centred, ruthless persona.

Lydia in contrast takes the same jovial and fun-loving outlook everywhere she goes and as a consequence plays her best golf when she is relaxed and happy. Leadbetter and his team, like Guy Wilson, David Niethe and Lydia's parents during her amateur career, work hard on creating an environment that keeps her light and laughing.

'I've never seen anything quite like her,' Leadbetter has commented. 'I've seen players who have a little bit of what she has but not everything. She's the full package. A great golfer, a great role model, somebody who doesn't have a mean bone in her body and someone who is a delight to be around . . . no matter what, Lydia does it with a smile. She is simply a treasure. She really is.'

On top of all this, or perhaps because of it, Lydia has a humility not often found in world-class athletes.

The only time anyone seemed remotely annoyed at Lydia's self-effacing nature came when Stacy Lewis, part tongue-in-cheek, called her out for being too humble.

'I think she knows how good she is, but I wish she would kind of own up to it sometimes, to say, "I'm the number one player in the world, and I'm pretty good." But she's really humble about it, and she doesn't really want anybody to think that about her.

'So it's almost frustrating in a way, because you want her just to be a little more confident in it and a little bit more, "I'm the best player here and I'm going to win." You know she's thinking that inside, but she doesn't really portray that.'

But is she thinking that inside? It's hard to tell, but Lydia's humility appears absolutely genuine and has as its wellspring the very deep understanding that golf is — as writer John Updike once described it — the only sport where a player can see room for 'infinite improvement'. She's humble because she understands the game is primarily a battle with herself to be the best she can be.

As a 16-year-old, Lydia told *Golf Digest*: 'I don't think I had a moment when I thought I was good — I was just having fun and when I play good it gives me confidence.

'I just want to become a better player — there's always something I can improve on — there's no perfect in the game and that's the beauty of golf, you always try to find something else. You always know there's a step further to climb and I hope I'm going up those stairs and not down.'

The other element of Lydia's personality that surprises those around her is her ability to act her age — to behave and react to situations as a teenager. Professional sport demands a lot of young players and it can make them cynical, guarded and world-weary in a short time. Yet Lydia has avoided falling victim to the soul-eating demands of life in a professional caravan.

Lydia's best friend on the tour is American Danielle Kang, whom Lydia describes as a 'middle sister' as she's slightly younger than her own big sister Sura Ko.

The pair can often be found in each other's social posts and started a (now dormant) YouTube channel called KangKoLPGA with videos of them singing, lounging around the airport and wishing 'Happy Birthday' to Danielle's mum. They epitomise having fun.

Danielle has known Lydia since she was 13 and has said she's the same easy-going person now as she was then: 'She's still just Lydia. She's still normal, there's nothing extravagant. She's not any different than when she was thirteen. She just goes with the flow, she's very calm but when she needs to do something she'll get it done.'

Her sunny disposition has an effect on those around her.

They are drawn in by her energy and aura.

LPGA commissioner Mike Whan was so inspired by the way she presents herself, he said: 'When I'm really miserable on a golf course, I try to channel my inner Lydia and smile my way through my triple bogeys.'

Karen Crouse of the *New York Times*, one of the most respected feature writers in American sport, spent a day watching Lydia on the golf course and wrote: 'To fully appreciate what makes Ko special, it helps to see her in person, because her charisma cannot be captured in the quick cutaway shots that make up televised golf coverage.' She added: 'Ko will laugh or make a funny face or gesture so animatedly that fans in her gallery, magnetised by her personality, will lean in her direction.'

Others have compared her to one of the greats of the men's game, Arnold Palmer, who was the ultimate man of the people. Friendly, charming, polite and funny, Palmer popularised golf in the 1950s and '60s, attracting a huge following of supporters known as Arnie's Army. Fan-friendly, well-mannered, unrelentingly upbeat and funny in her dry Kiwi way, Lydia is the modern female version of Palmer.

Despite all her success and the praise heaped on her, Lydia never gets big-headed or full of herself. 'She has that gift of treating the regular people like superstars and the superstars like regular people,' said Meghan Flanagan, the LPGA's senior coordinator of tour media.

That was never more evident than when Lydia met Steph Curry, the biggest star in the world's biggest basketball show, the NBA. The Golden State Warriors shooting machine met Lydia ahead of the Swinging Skirts event in San Francisco in 2016, and in a world where people would crawl across broken glass to spend time with Curry, it was the basketballer who lay at Lydia's feet like a puppy.

Curry, himself a pretty laidback customer, was in awe of Lydia, saying it was inspiring to meet a superstar who was 'so grounded . . . just seeing her attitude and temperament around this setting is pretty refreshing'.

Lydia recognises there is pressure on her shoulders — she knows she's expected to win, people are drawn to her, the media want a slice of her, children look up to her — but she is not driven by these expectations to be anything but who she is.

'All I can do is be myself — that's the best I can do, I can't portray myself as a different person to who I normally am and that's really important.'

There's no doubt Lydia's family has played a part in moulding her. A New Zealand Golf staffer described the Ko family as 'an impressive unit and Tina has done an incredible job with the kind of person Lydia is — she's appreciative, she gives back, she's a good human being'.

Michael Yim, Lydia's manager, a Korean-American who understands the cultural values instilled in Lydia by her parents, has said respect for others formed the core of her belief system.

'She is a very impressive person all around. Some of the things she thinks, says and does are really beyond her years. She is smart, funny, confident, youthful, caring, and mature all in one. What impresses me the most about her is how she respects people, whether it's kids or adults.'

What's clear is that Lydia doesn't want, or try, to be someone she isn't. Since she was a girl she's had a strong sense of self. She knows who she is and where she's going.

That applies both off and on the course. Her humility in life makes her humble in the face of the game — she understands she's not bigger than the game, that she's not more important than any of her rivals who give meaning to a contest, that she owes thanks to sponsors for making tournaments possible, that she respects fans for shelling out their hard-earned cash to watch her play. She realises golf is not played in a vacuum and that all she's achieved wouldn't be possible without the input of millions of people, from her parents to her social media fans.

And the twist is that the game of golf only reinforces those values.

Emily Perry, her former teammate and fellow student of psychology, says the fact Lydia has played golf without fear or insecurity, that she's tackled the game with the determination to have fun, has shaped her as a person.

'In the sports world,' Emily says, 'people talk about their rivals and try to bring them down. It's competition, people are there to win, but with her you know no matter what you do, she's going to do her own thing and not waste any time being nasty.'

American psychiatrist M Scott Peck, who was also a golfer, says in his book *Golf and the Spirit: Lessons for the Journey* that he cannot think of any game better calculated to teach the spiritual virtues we need to learn: 'humility, patience, precision, balance, and alertness, as well as the never-ending practice of kenosis [that is, self-emptying; letting go of ego-control].'

For most, it's a matter of learning about life through golf. Lydia, on the other hand, arrived at golf with many of the life lessons already learned. It made her a better golfer, which in turn made her a better person.

'She's a special human being,' says mental trainer David Niethe. 'She has a special gift for a game that is world-renowned and we've all been blessed because of her.'

Niethe says the team drawn together around Lydia — from her parents, to Guy Wilson, to others like himself at the Institute of Golf, to New Zealand Golf, to her backers and friends — could all see a unique energy in their pupil.

'We just knew — I can't explain it or define it, and there's almost a spiritual element to it . . . but we just knew, we all recognised, and had a mutual respect for, the gift we'd been given.'

Chapter Eighteen
Secrets revealed

From the 18th fairway of the Mission Hills Country Club in Rancho Mirage, California, Lydia's eyes follow her ball like a hawk, watching intently as it lands on the green exactly where her caddy Jason Hamilton has told her to hit it. It lands, skips and stops about half a metre left of the hole to create an easy birdie putt.

Lydia twirls in the fairway, acknowledges the applause of the fans with the wave of her glove; and her self-effacing smile reflects the simple joy of having conjured up and sculpted a thing of beauty.

The birdie putt falls, leaving Lydia at 12 under par and in the lead in the final round of the ANA Inspiration, the first major of 2016 in late March.

But she must wait to see what the young Thai player, Ariya Jutanugarn, will do. If the big-hitter can make a birdie she can tie Lydia and force a play-off. If not, Lydia will become the youngest woman in history to win two major championships, surpassing the feat of Korean legend Se Ri Pak. She will also be the first 18-year-old in almost 150 years — male or female — to win multiple major championships.

She is on the verge of golf immortality. She has done all she can do — the rest is out of her control.

Just as Lydia survived the trial by fire to set up her birdie putt on the last hole, Ariya feels the weight of pressure as she stands on the 18th tee.

The possibility of winning her first major hangs heavily on the young Thai's strong shoulders. She held a healthy lead a few holes earlier but successive bogeys on the 16th and 17th means she is level with Lydia as she stands on the tee.

Pressure causes strange things to happen to a player's body — the muscles tense, it feels hard to take a deep breath, an easy-going rhythm a few holes ago is snatched away and replaced by a quick rip. Under the heat of battle Ariya melted — her tee shot on the 18th spiralled left and into the water and with it drowned her hopes of winning.

Throughout the day Lydia had clawed and scraped to stay in the contest, needing to make a series of nerve-wracking putts to stay in touch with the leaders. But when the hardest question of the day was asked, when she wriggled into a position to win the tournament, she recalibrated from survival to attack.

Victory at the ANA Inspiration is celebrated with a ceremonial dive into a greenside lake known as Poppie's Pond.

The strange ritual started in 1988 when Amy Alcott, overcome with excitement at winning, plunged into the water, which is about 1.5 metres deep. From gentle flops to tentative wading in the early days, the players now get more and more extravagant with their running dives — and Lydia was no different, holding her hands above her head in her favourite heart shape as she led her mother Tina, sister Sura, caddy Jason and his fiancée in a team plunge.

Afterwards, wearing a white robe to keep warm, she agreed the shot to the 18th green ranked as the best of her short but spectacular career. 'Every shot is special in its own way, like every win is special, because every tournament is so different, but just playing the seventy-second hole, birdieing the last hole, that's always a good feeling. Obviously for that shot to mean so much that I would win the event, that makes it extra special. [I] hit it to the exactly right spot. It ended up being perfect.'

Discussing Lydia's performance afterwards, John Cook, one of the few professionals to have a close friendship with Tiger Woods, compared the young Kiwi sensation to the greatest male player of the past 20 years.

'There are similarities to Tiger Woods,' Cook said on Golf Channel, 'that inner drive, the will to compete — the wanting to be the best — you see that in Lydia, you saw it in Tiger and not many have that ability to reach that far deep inside them to be that great.'

Seemingly immune to pressure, Lydia's ability to conjure up miracles had Randall Mell of Golf Channel joking that instead of the ceremonial dive into Poppie's Pond 'the only reason she didn't walk across Poppie's Pond is because she thought it would make her look like she was showing off'.

In winning her second major championship three weeks before she turned 19, Lydia — again — rewrote history.

In what's known as the modern era of golf (post-1900), she became the youngest — by some margin, male or female — to win two major championships, surpassing the legendary Gene

Sarazen, who was 20 years, 5 months and 22 days old when he won his second major in 1922, as well as surpassing her role model and inspiration Se Ri Pak, who was 20 years, 9 months and 8 days old when she won her second major in 1998.

Only Young Tom Morris, who won his second British Open when he was 18, in 1869, is a younger multiple major winner.

A few weeks later, on the day Lydia turned 19, her record on the LPGA Tour was almost beyond comprehension: 74 tournaments, 73 cuts made, 45 top-10 finishes, 12 wins and 2 majors.

By comparison, at a similar stage in his career — 74 tournaments on the PGA Tour, including some as an amateur — Tiger Woods' record was: 74 tournaments, 63 cuts made, 33 top-10s, 9 wins, and 1 major.

For all she's done as a teenager, there is much more to accomplish for Lydia. Landmarks stretch out in front her: some attainable, some with question marks over them.

The most major wins by a woman belongs to Patty Berg, with 15 accrued between 1937 and 1958. The most wins on the LPGA Tour is 88 by Kathy Whitworth, compiled over a 23-year period from 1962 to 1985.

The only thing that could seemingly stop Lydia surpassing these marks is her oft-repeated assertion that she will retire when she's 30, meaning a 14-year professional career. It's feasible she could match Berg's major mark, but another 76 wins to match Whitworth over the next 11 years seems inconceivable.

And there's no guarantee she will keep winning . . . Lydia's rise to the top of the world coincided with the spectacular decline of Taiwan's Yani Tseng, who won five major championships before she was 22 and held the world No. 1 ranking for 109 weeks from 2008 to 2011.

But Yani hasn't won since 2012 and has plummeted down

the rankings. Speculation on the reasons for her precipitous decline include a view that once she got to the top of the world she looked around and saw there was another life to enjoy away from golf. But, based on what's she's revealed, it appears she suffered a mental disintegration so complete she simply forgot how to play golf. And — importantly — forgot how to enjoy herself.

'Things are very easy to get in your mind, especially when you're doubting yourself,' she has said.

Tseng hired Bob Rotella as her mental coach and he locked on to some of the very things Lydia has astutely avoided so far in her career.

'Yani said she felt like when she was winning everything, she didn't know a whole lot about golf,' Rotella said. 'She was just picturing a shot and ripping it. She was just having fun, and she said: "They just kept handing me trophies and cheques, and then when everyone started telling me how much potential I had, it started to change everything." She said she started getting more serious, trying to do everything perfectly. And then she started feeling pressure, and she got lost.'

One thing that will help ensure Lydia avoids the same downspiral as Yani is the fact her caddy Jason Hamilton was Tseng's long-time bag carrier at the time of her demise, eventually getting the sack as she struggled to work out what had gone wrong.

So what is the secret to Lydia Ko's success? What has made her the best teenage golfer in the long and illustrious history of the game?

It's a question Lydia has been asked many times and her usual answer is something like this: 'I don't think there is like this secret. And I think people have asked me this, and kind of think there is something behind it, but I personally don't know what is doing this. But the big thing is I'm having lots of fun. I wouldn't be able to tell you this magical secret and equation behind things.'

Maybe the answer is that a range of factors have all contributed.

She was born in the right place, at the right time. Coming into the world in the late 1990s in South Korea, Lydia was born into a society where Se Ri Pak's heroics inspired a generation of golfers. Heroes and role models are vital in connecting children to a sport. Heroes spark the love that produces the intrinsic motivation.

Lydia's Korean heritage cannot be overlooked or downplayed, but more influential than the discipline and drive and the so-called Korean work ethic is the fact her parents were supportive, nurturing and prepared to make huge sacrifices for the benefit of their daughter.

With the parental sacrifice came the obligation for Lydia to give back; it's asking a lot of a child to understand they owe a debt to their parents but it also seems to be a fair trade. Perhaps those who say modern children are too indulged have a point — as a child Lydia understood she had a responsibility to hold up her side of the golf bargain.

Coaching is critical, and it has to be proper coaching, as opposed to having a well-meaning parent, friend or volunteer try to instil basics. Lydia's parents were prepared to pay a modest sum for Guy Wilson's services but it returned a massive dividend.

Lydia learned the game from green to tee, honing the smaller shots before learning how to hit the ball greater distances. She mastered the scoring shots first.

Hitting thousands upon thousands of golf balls is critical,

Lydia's Korean heritage cannot be overlooked or downplayed, but more influential than the discipline and drive and the so-called Korean work ethic is the fact her parents were supportive, nurturing and prepared to make huge sacrifices.

but it should not be mindless repetition; each shot should have a purpose. Adaptation and versatility, though, are just as important as repetition for developing skills. Lydia's father tested her mind as much as her mechanics.

A plan with long-term goals — looking 10 or even 20 years ahead — is vital. Dream goals may initially seem so far away as to be implausible, but as they get closer the focus can sharpen. Lydia dreamt about being a top professional when she was as young as seven. Within a few years that dream had solidified into an attainable vision.

Her rivalries were all positive. From Cecilia Cho to Inbee Park, her fellow competitors brought out the best in her; she chased them without needing to bring them down.

Mental skills are as important as physical skills — possibly more important — and can be learned from a young age. Learning how to separate physical outcomes of a golf shot from an emotional reaction meant Lydia was never negative or angry with herself. This allowed her to maintain confidence and a positive self-image.

She also learned to embrace pressure, to understand it was part of the game, rather than fight it or fear it.

And, as trite as it might sound, she is doing something she loves. Sport is a serious business but sometimes it is taken too seriously. As in life, if a person can find a career they enjoy, it never feels like work.

The results — from a technical point of view — are there for everyone to see. She drives the ball accurately thanks to a repeatable swing with a constant rhythm and easy tempo; her short irons are immaculate in terms of distance control and accuracy thanks to Guy Wilson's determination to teach these basics first. Her putting is sometimes — only sometimes — a minor liability, but she gives herself more birdie chances than most players because of her unerring accuracy. When she's on song with the putter she will always be in contention.

On the psychological side, her temperament and demeanour are impeccable. She has the ability to execute under pressure, to maintain her beautiful swing tempo without tensing up and becoming too quick, to think clearly when the heat is on, to not react negatively or emotionally to bad shots, nor get over-excited by the good shots. She's not immune to pressure — she feels it — she just has an ability to control it.

Much of how she is on the golf course mentally seems to be the personification of the behaviours described in Bob Rotella's seminal book on golf psychology: *Golf is Not a Game of Perfect.*

Rotella stresses that having fun, separating emotion from the technical aspects of the game, enjoying the simple pleasure of being in the fresh air, walking on finely manicured grass (the opposite to Mark Twain's oft-quoted 'golf is a good walk spoiled'), not overthinking but playing with flow, not fearing failure, learning the game from close to the green by ingraining chipping and putting . . . in short she has the perfect psychological make-up for the game. It's almost as if Rotella's book is her bible.

Plenty of people have read Rotella's books over the past 20 years but Lydia appears to be the one who truly plays by his rules.

But that's not the entire answer.

Something else sets her apart from all the others with their perfect swings, long hours of practice, supportive parents, astute coaches, meticulous plans, mental trainers and positive outlook.

Across Auckland, and around the world, there are Korean families contemplating how they can turn their daughter into the next Lydia Ko. As one of these dads noted: 'Other parents are hopeful and we have to remain hopeful . . . but Lydia is one in a billion.'

Perhaps this last point is the most salient in trying to define why Lydia — and not one of the many other Se Ri kids of her generation with similar backgrounds and upbringing — is the top of the world. While others tried to replicate what worked for Se Ri, Lydia took inspiration from her hero but found her own unique path, some of it by chance. The family came to New Zealand instead of Canada; Guy Wilson just happened to be working in the Pupuke pro shop when Lydia came in; the Institute of Golf was formed just as she was hitting her straps; she had a series of inspirational rivals placed in her path . . . all of it adds up like building blocks.

But, still, there's something else.

While shaped and nurtured by so many people — most especially her parents, who deserve all the kudos in the world for raising such a wonderful person — Lydia possesses an innate quality, a gift, that cannot be captured on a Trackman monitor, downloaded from YouTube, isolated in endless statistics, heard in a victory speech or found in a Perspex box of cash.

It's in her snaggle-toothed smile, her natural humility, her face as it concentrates on a shot, her generosity, the way she walks, her boundless positive energy, her off-beat sense of humour, her open-heartedness, her ability to turn challenges into opportunities, her imagination and her ability to see the world as a fun place to be . . . in the end, or rather the beginning, there's a phrase numerous people have used when contributing to this book:

She was just born Lydia.

Acknowledgements

A number of people were very generous with their time, support and help on the direction of this book.

Emily Perry, a former New Zealand teammate and rival of Lydia's, and who is now a student of psychology, was insightful, engaging and enthusiastic and offered critical insights into Lydia's personality and mental drive.

That understanding was augmented by David Niethe — a welcoming, warm and entertaining story-teller. His unparalleled grasp of how Lydia's mind works was invaluable in charting the direction of this book.

Ryan Fox, amid a hectic schedule, took time out to share his memories of growing up in the golf world alongside Lydia.

A number of former journalist colleagues were amazing sources of information about Lydia's earlier career, having been on the ground at tournaments and practice sessions, so a big shout out to Simon Plumb of NZME, Fred Woodcock of Fairfax NZ and Peter Thornton.

Ken Hodge offered thoughtful academic rigour around sports psychology. Paul Spoonley provided vital background on the patterns of Asian immigration and Auckland's changing demographics. Jay Waters was enthusiastic and supportive of this project and allowed me to fully understand how modern transnational Korean families operate.

John Lister was a great raconteur with a deep understanding of professional golf and his recollections of mentoring a young Lydia Ko added depth to the book.

Pam Greenhalgh and Andrew Leventis of North Harbour Golf were enthusiastic and magnanimous.

I'd particularly like to thank Phil Hamilton for his endless listening to my stories of Lydia as we played our regular Monday round of golf at Titirangi — his golfing intelligence was a great sounding board.

Glossary

Approach: shot into the green.

Back nine: the second nine holes of a golf course.

Birdie: completing the hole in one shot less than par; e.g. making a three on a par-four.

Bogey: completing the hole in one shot more than par (a double bogey is two shots over par, a triple bogey is three shots over par, etc.).

Break: how much a putt will curve on its way to the hole.

Bunkers/sand traps: pits filled with sand and generally incorporating a raised lip or barrier, from which the ball is more difficult to play than from grass.

Carry: how far a ball has to travel in the air to avoid an obstacle; e.g. 'he had 200 metres to carry the bunker at the front of the green'.

Chip: a very short shot from just off the green.

Cut: after two rounds of a tournament, the players below a certain score or position are eliminated. Usually the top 60 'make the cut' for weekend play while those below that mark 'miss the cut'.

Draw: a shot that bends right to left (for a right-hander).

Drive: shot with a driver — the first shot on a hole.

Driver: the longest club, with the biggest head, designed to hit the ball the greatest distance.

Eagle: completing the hole in two shots under par; e.g. making a three on a par-five (a double eagle, or albatross, is three shots under par).

Fade: a shot that gently moves left to right (for a right-hander).

Fairway: closely mown, defined area of the course.

Front nine: the first nine holes of a golf course.

Green: tightly mown, clearly defined, rolled surface where the hole is located.

Hazard: obstacles such as bunkers, creeks (burns) and lakes designed to penalise a player for a bad stroke.

Irons (one iron through to nine iron): series of clubs with blade-like heads and increasing angles of loft designed to hit shots of different distances and with different levels of backspin. A nine iron goes higher in the air and covers a shorter distance than an eight iron, and so on. The one to four irons are known as long irons; five to seven are mid-irons; eight and nine are short irons.

Lay-up: a second shot on a par-five, also used to describe a shot where a player deliberately plays short of the green to avoid trouble such as a creek or a bunker.

Lie: where the ball is sitting; e.g. a ball in the rough can be said to have a bad lie.

Loft: the angle of the club face that controls trajectory and affects distance achieved.

LPGA: Ladies Professional Golf Association.

Majors: the premier tournaments every year: for women, there are five: the ANA Inspiration, Women's PGA, US Open,

British Open and Evian Championship.

Match play: players are matched in head-to-head contests (either in singles or pairs), where the result is measured by holes won as opposed to strokes taken.

Par: completing the hole in the designated number of shots.

Par-three: a hole designed to be completed in three shots — a tee shot and two putts.

Par-four: a hole designed to be completed in four shots — a tee shot, an approach to the green and two putts. A driveable par-four is a hole where a player can reach the green in one shot.

Par-five: a hole designed to be completed in five shots — a tee shot, a lay-up, an approach and two putts. Many par-five holes can be 'reached' in two shots. A player who attacks a par-five in such a fashion is described as 'going for it' in two.

Pin, pin position, flag: terms used to designate where on the green the hole is located.

Pitch: a short aerial shot — generally less than 45 metres (50 yards) from the green.

Putt: a shot along the ground with a putter.

Putter: flat-faced club for rolling the ball on the surface of the green.

Read: to study the slopes and contours of a green to estimate how much a putt will break (curve).

Rough: longer, thicker grass on the edges of the fairway designed to make it harder for the player to make clean contact with the ball.

Shape: the line traced by a golf ball in flight relating to whether it curves and how high or low it goes.

Stroke play: where players compete to finish the tournament in the fewest strokes.

Tee: the position from which players start a hole.

Three-putt: taking three putts to get the ball in the hole once the green has been attained — regarded as a bad mistake for professionals.

Tour: a season-long series of events under the jurisdiction of the LPGA.

Wedge (noun): clubs (pitching wedge, sand wedge, lob wedge) with a high degree of loft designed for pinpoint accuracy and maximum spin to stop the ball quickly on the green. Wedges are also referred to in terms of loft — 56-degree wedge, 60-degree wedge, 64-degree wedge, reflecting the angle of the club face.

Wedge (verb): to hit a short shot into the green (in the region of 45–90 metres/50–100 yards).

Wood (three-wood, five-wood): club with a slightly smaller head than a driver, and with a more lofted face, designed to hit long distances from the fairway.

Yardage: distance from the ball's current position to the desired finishing point on the fairway or green.